Advance Reviews Of

Success Briefs For Lawyers:

Inspirational Insights On How To Succeed At Law And Life

"I found the book to be both inspiring and instructional. The stories in the book enhanced my pride in being a member of the legal profession and reminded me about the great opportunities that exist within our community to serve as role models for others."

Lawrence J. Center, Executive Director of CLE
Georgetown University Law Center

"Many lawyers need to slow down and reflect, and even though we should know why, this collection tells us in many delightful ways. From wonderful role models and mentors, we now have personal reflections to learn from and make part of our journeys. There is humor, courage and peacemaking modeled for us. There is growing, changing and managing success, as well as images of leadership, integrity and adaptability."

H. James Hatch, III, Director
CLE Institute, Ohio State Bar Association

"Imagine leaving your briefcase unpacked and putting the journals and newspapers aside. Don't interrupt me now – I have to read! That was how I felt as I looked forward to reading this book. When you are inundated with the job at hand, here's a chance to return to the bigger ideas and ideals that we enjoyed thinking and talking about in law school. I particularly enjoyed the variety in this book: essays, autobiographical entries, wonderful quotations, even poetry: something for every mood and need."

Bernice A. Heilbrunn, Counsel
LYONDELL-CITGO Refining LP

"*Success Briefs for Lawyers* reminds the reader that there is more to life than the billable hour. It inspires the reader to follow a different path and it reassures the reader that the rewards awaiting us along that different path may be more dear than those we traditionally associate with the practice of law."

Mary Jane Trapp
Partner, Apicella & Trapp
President, Ohio State Bar Association

"The authors have delivered a page-turner that forces every lawyer to reexamine his or her priorities."

Robert L. Carter, Jr., Partner
McKenna & Cuneo

"Law is in a crisis. What lawyers desperately need is not yet another cry of alarm about the problems of the profession, but practical resources to help them deal with the crisis of identity and meaning that afflicts their work. That is what makes *Success Briefs for Lawyers* such an important book. It is chock-full of inspirational stories by real life lawyers who have found ways to bring a sense of meaning and purpose – and even joy – to their work. These stories can revitalize tired lawyers and give them a new vision of themselves and their work. This book is perfect for anyone who is a lawyer, wants to be a lawyer, or cares about a lawyer."

Joseph Allegretti
Author of "The Lawyer's Calling: Christian Faith and Legal Practice"

"*Success Briefs for Lawyers* is a reminder to all of us that balance is essential in our lives. This book provides us with concrete examples of lawyers who have learned that lesson – sometimes belatedly – and have improved their lives immeasurably. Unlike most self-help books, this one succeeds by having lawyers tell their own stories."

Marc L. Fleischaker, Partner and Chairman
Arent Fox Kintner Plotkin & Kahn, PLLC

"As I am not a lawyer, I will not urge that lawyers read this volume; as an educator, I will urge strongly that everyone read it and read it carefully. *Success Briefs for Lawyers* addresses universal problems and offers inspiration for any individual trying to live a fulfilling life. Indeed, its strength lies in its dual message – that a balanced life is possible while still making a difference."

Gregory S. Prince, Jr.
President of Hampshire College
Vice-Chair, ABA Council On
Racial And Social Justice

"I thoroughly enjoyed reading this book. I found it to be wonderfully uplifting. Not only does this book capture the pulse and ailments of the legal profession, but it offers insights, inspirations and treatments in a most delightful way. It is sure to produce conversation and creative thinking within a profession that truly can make a difference in the heart and soul of our American culture."

Susan D. Lengal, Exec. Director
Akron Bar Association

"*Success Briefs for Lawyers* is like a breath of fresh air. It is the story of individual lawyers who after reflecting their roles in the profession, rededicated themselves to the profession in a healthy, productive way. The book ought to be required reading for law students and new lawyers."

Steven C. Bahls, Dean
Capital University Law School

"Too many attorneys have lost sight of their professional calling. The essays and personal experiences collected here are refreshing and inspirational. While it would be nice to have this book read by every newly licensed lawyer, the restoration of the quality of life issues addressed by the authors will not occur until all of the managing partners and leaders in the profession have studied the essence of the book and taken it to heart."

Gerald L. Draper, Partner
Roetzel & Andress

"*Success Briefs for Lawyers* effectively reminds us that the motives, goals and talents of lawyers fall across a broad spectrum of human behavior. It also attests artfully to the ultimate irony of an attorney's life, that it is often easier to diagnose and solve the problems of others that to deal with one's own shortcomings."

Mark R. Steinberg
Partner, O'Melveny & Myers
Former Associate Deputy Attorney General
U.S. Department of Justice

"We hear and read so very much about the malaise and the active dissatisfaction with the profession that afflicts so many in the middle years that it is refreshing to see this collection of readable, palatable and effective ways to combat negative forces and restore balance, priority and perspective to one's professional and personal life."

William C. Becker, Director
Institute for Professional Responsibility
University of Akron School of Law

National Association For Public Interest Law

The editors and authors have agreed to create this book without compensation. Using the moneys that would have been spent on royalties, and adding its own contribution, the publisher will in turn donate 15% of the income derived from the sale of this book to the National Association for Public Interest Law (NAPIL).

NAPIL was founded in 1986 by law students dedicated to surmounting barriers to equal justice that affect millions of low-income individuals and families. Today, NAPIL is the country's leading organization engaged in organizing, training and supporting public service-minded law students, and is the national leader in creating summer and postgraduate public interest jobs.

Contributions are accepted at: NAPIL, 2120 L Street, NW, Suite 450 Washington, DC 20037, (202) 466-3686 / Fax (202) 429-9766 - napil@napil.org.

Also by Amiram Elwork

Stress Management for Lawyers:
How To Increase Personal &Professional Satisfaction In The Law

SUCCESS BRIEFS FOR LAWYERS

Inspirational Insights On How To Succeed At Law And Life

Edited By

Amiram Elwork, Ph.D.
Law-Psychology Graduate Program
Widener University

Mark R. Siwik, J.D.
Risk International

The Vorkell Group
Gwynedd, Pennsylvania

Published By:
The Vorkell Group
P.O. Box 447, Gwynedd, PA 19436
Phone: (215) 661-9330; Fax: (215) 661-9328
Order Line: (800) 759-1222; Website: Vorkell.com

Printed in the United States of America
The Vorkell Group donates a portion of its book proceeds to charities.
Cover design by John Goschke, Cornerstone Media, Ambler, PA.

Publisher's Cataloging in Publication Data
(Provided by Quality Books, Inc.)

Elwork, Amiram
Success briefs for lawyers : inspirational insights on how to succeed at law and life / edited by Amiram Elwork, Mark R. Siwik. -- 1st ed.
p.cm.
LCCN: 00-104520
ISBN: 0-9644727-2-4

1. Lawyers--Conduct of life--Biography. 2.Practice of law--Biography. 3.Success. I. Siwik, Mark.R. II. Title

KF353.E49 2001 340.0922
QBI00-569

Amiram Elwork dedicates this book to his loving parents, Fania and Gregori Elwork. They inspired me to try to make the world a better place and modeled for me all there was to know about true success.

Mark Siwik dedicates this book to his loving grandmother, Anna C. Siwik. She was a common woman with an uncommon affection for and desire to help other people.

Acknowledgments

Creating this book has required the help of many people to whom we are very grateful. First and foremost, we want to thank our families: Andrea, Rachael, and Rebecca Elwork, and Lori, Melissa, and Maxwell Siwik. Thank you for your love, patience, and sacrifices. You support and sustain us.

We also want to thank our assistants, Gloria Patterson, Curt Gross, Adele Williams, and Heather Kelly, for helping us make all of the phone calls and write all of the letters. In addition, we want to thank Rachael Elwork, Daniel Glessner, Lisa Gradert, Greg Hadley, Linda Kersker, Andrew and Bena Paisley, Paul Rose, John Solomon and Martin Soniker for their valuable editorial comments.

Jim Hatch and Terrell Hunt also deserve our thanks for encouraging us to create this book. We also want to express our appreciation to our mentors: Ken Aplin, U.S. District Court Judge John M. Manos, Steve Petras, Paul Rose, and Bruce Sales.

This book would obviously not have been possible without our authors. Thank you for caring enough about the legal profession to want to give back to it. Finally, there are the attendees at our seminars whom we challenge to speak up and make a difference. Thank you for pushing us to do the same.

Contents

Some men see things as they are and say why. I dream things that never were and say why not?

Robert F. Kennedy

Introduction

Amiram Elwork* &
Mark R. Siwik†

Every year, we have the privilege of speaking to lawyers at seminars across the country about what is right and good in the legal profession and what they can do to be more effective and satisfied with their lives. A significant number of attorneys in our audiences are disbelieving and opine that little can be done to change things for the better. Sometimes, we even get looks typically reserved for crazed idealists.

We try to shift the tone in the room from negativity to genuine problem-solving by inviting members of the audience to share personal stories describing how they dealt with a difficult circumstance. The best moments at our seminars are when some lawyers actually admit to being happy with their careers and

---

* Dr. Amiram Elwork is the Director of the Law-Psychology (J.D.-Psy.D.) Graduate Program at Widener University, near Philadelphia, and he has a consulting practice that serves the legal community.

† Mark R. Siwik is Senior Counsel at Risk International Services, Inc., in Cleveland, Ohio, where he helps commercial policyholders resolve complex insurance claims. Mark also devotes substantial time to improving the legal profession.

lives, and then proceed to share their "secrets." These experiences have led us to conclude that the legal profession could benefit greatly from positive role models willing to share some of their hard-earned lessons about how best to live a lawyer's life. In essence, that is the reason we decided to create this collection of biographical essays.

We offer this book in stark contrast to much of what lawyers have typically read about their profession in the last decade of the 20th Century. It has been widely reported that there has been a significant deterioration of the legal work environment, a reduction in career satisfaction among lawyers, and a decrease in the physical and mental health of lawyers. Among the most often posited explanations for what is wrong with the practice of law today, is the charge that too many law firms are run like "businesses." The truth is, of course, that the practice of law has always been a business providing professional services. What critics truly mean is that too many lawyers have become overly materialistic and that other values are no longer as important as they once were during an era of "professionalism."

Materialism and a rapid increase in the number of lawyers in our society, have made the practice of law much more competitive than it was in the past. These forces have also created too many unhealthy legal work environments that reward workaholism above all else. In turn, this has given rise to a significant number of lawyers whose professional lives are out of balance with their personal lives. Additionally, the emphasis on materialism, competition, and work have contributed to a loss of civility, decency and morality in the legal profession.

In recognition of this problem, the legal community has taken a number of ameliorating steps in recent years. For example, bar associations have urged their members to get more involved in pure public service activities, and to get more ethical training in law school and beyond. Today, some jurisdictions require continuing legal education in alcoholism, substance abuse, mental health issues, and stress management. Their logic is that since mental health problems and ethical violations are often correlated, if one can be prevented then so will the other. Some of the most recent continuing legal education efforts attempt to improve the level of "professionalism" in the legal community by focusing on such basic values as integrity and civility.

Our book represents an attempt to contribute to these efforts in a different way. It is based on the idea that modeling is a highly effective behavioral tool, and that inspiration is a powerful motivator. Our reasoning is simple: If you want lawyers to achieve personal and professional satisfaction in the practice of law, find lawyers who have done it and learn from them. Positive role models not only prove that a good life is possible in the law, but they also teach us how to achieve it through the power of their example.

And so, a couple of years ago we started asking lawyers to send us their positive stories and lessons. We read countless magazine articles, talked with many lawyers, and mailed hundreds of letters in our quest for inspirational essays. Each potential author received the following instructions:

> *As you write your essay, story, or poem, remember that the goal of the book is to provide inspirational and instructive ideas to lawyers for achieving professional and personal success. Inspiration springs from heartfelt convictions and we encourage you to share your feelings. Allow yourself plenty of creative flexibility. Writings of this type often evolve into something other than what was originally planned. It may take us a couple of rewrites before we both agree that the essay is ready for print, but hopefully the lasting and meaningful effect that your chapter can have will be well worth the effort.*

The rest of this book presents the cream of the crop of submissions we received. They represent a cross-section of lawyers from all regions of the United States with varying backgrounds and personal histories. While the specific lessons and advice they offer are wide ranging, their underlying messages are the same: at the core, a contented life usually depends on the extent to which a person's attained goals are in harmony with an internalized set of good values. In other words, the real winners in this world are people who strive to express the best of what is already inside of themselves.

It is our hope that this book may help to attract young people to the law for the right reasons, uplift the spirits of experienced lawyers in their dark moments, and present a more accurate and positive image of the profession to the public.

We know that the authors of the chapters that follow will make you think, tug your heartstrings, and tickle your funny bone. In addition, however, we hope that they will help bring out the best of what is already inside of you. If that happens, we will have truly succeeded. Together, we then have a chance to improve the legal profession.

One of the most attractive things about the flowers is their beautiful reserve.

Henry David Thoreau

Justice Mom & Her Flowers

Evelyn Lundberg Stratton*

Identity

Attorney/woman
Stalking courtroom corridors
Briefcase badge of identity
Clutched tightly to side
Severe blue suit
Quoting legal principles
Fierce in cross-examination
Fearless

Mother/woman
Rocking gently in a darkened room
Tiny head rests softly against her robe
Guilt brushed aside
Cruel, hard world locked out of thought and mind
Protect my child
Fearful.

---

* Justice Evelyn Lundberg Stratton serves on the Supreme Court of Ohio. She was formerly a trial attorney and trial judge. She is active in community charities, serving on the boards of Prevent Blindness Ohio and the Dave Thomas Adoption Foundation, while raising two teenage sons.

I am a child again. My memories take me back to my youth. The air is heavy, humid, wrapping me in its sticky envelope. I sit on the hard cement floor, outside the inner sanctum of the temple. It looms large about me, drowned by its glittering roof. I am not allowed in.

My father sits with the Buddhist priest, cross-legged, Thai style. He is patiently explaining the Christian faith. The priest shifts in his saffron robes, orange against the cool interior. He questions, probes, and challenges. His life is spent in an eternal quest for truth and understanding. He is fascinated by the Western religion. He shakes his head at our system where we sin and ask forgiveness. Theirs is a life of balance. If their good merits outweigh their bad deeds, they are reincarnated into a higher plane.

A soft breeze cools my brow as I rest my head against my arms, waiting. But here there is no rush. The Thai do not hurry. Time is endless. There is nowhere else to go. The search for truth knows no clock.

I snap back to the present, to the hard pew. The minister is droning on, it is 12:20. The roast may soon be overcooked; we have to eat by 1:30 to make football practice. I tap my watch impatiently.

I drift again to the memories of my childhood friend, a missionary kid like me, who shared with me how she was envious of me as a child because our parents put us first. We were away at missionary boarding school nine months each year, but when we came home to Thailand, my parents always carved out vacation time at a little bungalow on the Thai beach. I think of my father pulling me through the crashing waters, laughing, clapping.

It makes me think of another father, an attorney in a former pretrial, bragging about how he worked so hard, he hadn't had a vacation with the family in three years. Seeking sympathy, he moaned about getting home by 9 or 10 p.m. every night. I wonder about him; are his clients so much more important to him than his family? Does he ever spend time in his big fancy house? Do the kids want the big house more than their Dad? He seeks sympathy; I feel only pity for his family.

The preacher's words catch my attention, "Say no to temptation," he intones. Maybe saying no is the secret – I muse – no to the temptation of the extra dollar, that new committee, if the no means yes to the family. I shake my head – a tough word, "no." I have to practice it constantly, or else my public life will consume my private life. I hear myself apologizing to my son about why I can't make his final football game. If only I had apologized instead to that group begging me to speak to them. It made me feel so important. Now, I feel guilty. I must do better in meeting my goal of only being away one night per week and one weekend night per month. I must say "no" to the rest so I can be home more often. I must remind my secretary to be a tougher guardian of my time, to lecture me when I waiver.

The preacher has shifted to the last part of his sermon, which is on friendship. I think back to the Thai friends of my youth, never too busy or rushed to spend time with me, offering me a Thai meal of steaming spicy curries, stopping their work in the rice fields to while away the afternoon, sitting on their mats on the open porch, just reveling in the pleasure of visiting together. Such gracious hosts, generous with the gift of time. I make a mental note to add Lisa to my list of calls. I want to nurture friendships. There is never enough time, but I must make time.

The sermon is over and people pile out, jostling, rushing, and exchanging hurried pleasantries. I can walk home; I round the corner to my small house, a cottage some call it, filled with flowers in every corner. This is my personal haven. "Mom and her flowers," my kids say tolerantly. It is the place where I have time to myself, a chance to relish my moment of peace, and create color and life in a job often filled with sadness, pain, and death. Perhaps the tropical paradise of my youth inspires me.

I stop and look at my little house. I pause and reflect. I could have stayed in private practice, made three times my income, had all those fancy things. But, with all the grueling demands and long hours of a trial practice, could I still be Mom and really be there for my children? I can now make each drum lesson, every choir concert. Sure, I drag my briefs with me, but I'm there. And, I have a job that is so satisfying. I feel that I really contribute to society; that's worth more than possessions to me.

This society of more, bigger, and faster is so different from the simpler life of my Thai youth. The Thai didn't know the luxuries of our culture, but there was a contentment and peace in the Thai people that seems to be missing from the hustle and bustle of American life. I think it may be balance.

I reflect on the balance of the people of my childhood, the memories of priests in saffron robes, in early morning mist, passing from home to home with their rice bowl, collecting food. The Thai balance out their bad deeds for that week, or store up some extra credit, making merit by giving food to the priests.

How do I achieve balance in this hectic American society? Mother, wife, justice, community activist? What am I at any given moment? What is my identity?

My identity is that I am all those things, shifting from role to role, but always trying to keep my balance. Perhaps that is the influence of the Thai, the good merit balanced against life's missteps, the Yin and the Yang.

I think of this as my "Year of the Children." They are now teenagers, but somehow I find they need me more than ever. They don't want to *do* anything with me, but they want me *there*. And so I can plant my flowers and tend my garden with greater gusto, but I am there to drive them to football practice or to the card store. I do not mind playing the chauffeur; it is a quiet moment of captivity in a car where my sons talk to me, instead of just rushing by.

To keep that balance and to hold tight to my identity, I often do a self-check: Is my family suffering? Is my husband feeling neglected? Am I accepting too many speaking engagements? Are the boards too numerous? Which organization needs me most? Where can I be more valuable in my particular role as Justice?

I recently resigned from a prestigious board. I had a moment of simple clarity at a board meeting. As I sat there, eating a catered meal in a private dining room, looking around at the "who's who" cast of board members, I realized that they really didn't need me. My title was just a nice bonus on their letterhead. Everyone else there could provide the firepower. Yet my title could really open doors on another board, helping abused and neglected children. This was a board that couldn't attract the stellar board members because it wasn't politically popular. That board needed my time and willingness to work with them, not just my title. And so my choice suddenly became clear and easy. Where would I find the time to give the extra effort? I just found it. The balance shifted slightly, but harmony in my life was restored.

I have learned to carve out time in my work day. I make phone calls early in the morning when most are still in. I use e-mail to best convey details and information. I make time to read without interruption, and to just do "riff-raff" – that list of little tasks that accumulate in a pile such as a thank you letter or note to a colleague. I sift through mindless junk mail while I am on hold on the telephone.

I make my list for the day, and what is not done goes to the top of the next day's list. I practice delayed gratification. I do those unpleasant tasks first which sometimes take so much less time than you feared, that you wonder why you didn't tackle it sooner! That way, the pleasant tasks are your reward and make the day seem more manageable.

Oh yes, I have my lists. It is how I organize my life, fractured as it is, with its compartments. I keep a page for each facet of my life: committees, work projects, home projects, gifts to buy, and people to call for lunch. As each item comes up, I list it on the page in its category. Then, I no longer worry about trying to remember it. I receive great satisfaction each day as I review my lists, crossing out items and making a new "must do today" list. It keeps my entire life together. My husband laughs at my lists but humors me. He keeps his all in his head.

To save time, I also indulge in the luxury of having my law clerks drive me. It is a quiet time to discuss cases, to work on briefs uninterrupted, and to arrive alive because I didn't try to drive and talk on the cell phone! I encourage my busy business friends who drive a lot to hire a college kid to drive them. What they would pay out would come back full measure because they would extend their time.

Time-extenders are a way to steal those extra moments. As I drive alone, or tend my flowers, or clean the house, I often listen to books on tape, sometimes motivational, sometimes educational, and often for pure pleasure. Sometimes I cherish the pure silence of the garden, interrupted only by the band practice blaring from the garage. Books on tape are an American luxury that I have come to appreciate.

I am sure the Thai had no such need for these modern skills! If the rice needed planting when the monsoon rains fell, it was planted. It was harvested when ripe and golden. They have no need for lists and time-management skills. But alas, I am no longer in Thailand. I am a Justice on the Supreme Court of Ohio and must practice these skills to achieve that Yin and Yang. Perhaps this is more like the self-discipline of the martial arts!

And so, like the Thai, I seek the perfect balance, that certain harmony that brings peace, contentment, and fulfillment. I give and take, adjust and prioritize, and sometimes make difficult choices. Occasionally I forego planting the extra flower bed, when my relationship with my husband and children needs more nurturing. It *is* possible to have all those things in this busy, complicated world.

For the Thai, when the rains come, the entire family works knee deep in the muddy fields, planting each individual tender green seedling stalk of rice. In the hot, dry months while the rice grows silently, there is time for festivals, family, and visits on the open porch. So must I sometimes plant my seeds at work and in my garden, and sometimes I must simply sit back and watch them grow. For those vines weave together to form the pattern of my life and give me my identity.

If I had no sense of humor, I would long ago have committed suicide.

Mahatma Gandhi

My Name Is Ray And I Am An Alcoholic Lawyer

Ray O'K.[*]

At one of the Alcoholics Anonymous (AA) meetings I attended recently in North Carolina, where I live, a fellow stood up and said with a strong local accent, "Brothers and sisters, because of this AA program, the support of people like you, and God almighty, I have not found it necessary to have a drink since November 25th, 1965." After the applause died down, another guy stood up and said, "You're a liar, George. I saw you get drunk just last Tuesday." "I know," George answered, "I am just saying that it wasn't *necessary*."

Why did I start with that story? Obviously, I hope that the smile it puts on your face will entice you to read the rest of this essay. However, the story also serves to point out how difficult a problem alcoholism is. It is the underlying cause of a significant

---

[*] Ray O'K. is an Emeritus Professor of Law, having taught at Fordham University School of Law, Pace University School of Law, Thomas Cooley Law School, and St. Thomas University School of Law. He is a retired Justice of the Justice Court of the State of New York, and was a trial lawyer for thirty years.

proportion of malpractice and ethical violation cases against attorneys throughout our country, and it deserves our attention. In addition, I think that the high incidence of alcoholism among lawyers suggests that there may be something deeply wrong with our profession today.

I don't claim to have any special expertise on these matters, but having struggled with my own alcoholism for many years, I have come to some conclusions that work for me. With your indulgence, I will share them with you in the hope that they may help you or someone you know. Before imposing my conclusions on you, however, let me begin by telling you my story.

I was born and raised in one of the boroughs in New York City, called the Bronx. My neighborhood of South Bronx was rough, tough, and Irish. Drinking was very common both in my family and in my neighborhood. In psycho-babble terms, let's just say that I was the product of a dysfunctional family, living in a dysfunctional community.

I got my early education in the parochial school system. Where else would an Irish kid go? I hear people knocking Catholic schools, but I am very grateful to them. They educated me for free for many years and they also saved me from going blind. The latter benefit is a big item and something you don't ever forget.

I recall going into bars since I was thirteen years old. Before that, we drank without going into bars. I drank through all of high school and was thrown out several times for excessive drinking. As a matter of fact, I held the neighborhood record for being thrown out of high school, a record previously established by my brother Billy.

Nevertheless, I still went to college. Not only did I go to college, but I went to college in the state of Vermont. To a person from the Bronx, Vermont is a third world country. For an alcoholic, it was like going to a gulag. This place had no saloons. People drank in restaurants instead; they sat around tables and drank beers out of bottles. In addition, they sang college songs and wore white shoes in the wintertime.

Being a young man of no particular moral fiber, I got a pair of white shoes and started singing those dopey songs myself. For a while, things were going great. Eventually, however, I got into trouble with the school and the police, and decided to straighten things out by joining the Navy.

I hate to be indelicate, but my kidneys caused trouble for me in the Navy. You see, we slept three to a tier in the Navy, and the new guy slept on top. Once, after I got back to the ship drunk, I had one of those bed-wetting accidents. When I met the fellow who slept below me, he gently explained to me that while he expected to get wet sometime during his naval career, it had not occurred to him that it would happen while he was sleeping. I was immediately transferred to the lower bunk.

The rest of my career in the navy was equally distinguished. Three years later, I returned back to the neighborhood. Soon, I became engaged with some of my boyhood companions in forming a stolen car ring. As one would hope, I was to be the ring's chief executive. After spending about three days of planning the stolen car company, however, I suddenly had one of those clear thoughts that come to you once in a millennium.

I recalled that I had been to college once and could go back to finish. So, I got on a bus and arrived back in Vermont in the middle of a blizzard. Nothing had changed and no one had moved. They were all sitting around their restaurant tables just as before, singing songs in their white shoes.

Now, a grateful government was sending me monthly checks to go to school. Since I was moderately solvent, I got drunk much of the time. As a result, my college years are just a big blur to me. Nonetheless, I somehow managed to graduate from college, which was a first in our family.

My mother came north to participate in the tender occasion of my graduation. Some years later, when I became a trustee of the college, I noticed that they were still talking about my mother's visit. It isn't often in the state of Vermont that they see a little old lady get off the train drunk at nine o'clock in the morning, and then start a fistfight with the baggage guy.

Not only did I manage to graduate from college, but I also was able to get a scholarship to go to law school at Fordham University. Even though I had never met a lawyer and it proved to my family that I was not going to amount to anything, I went off to law school anyway. There were a lot of cops and priests in my neighborhood, but very few lawyers.

Law school scared the hell out of me and I went on the wagon. Except for the summers, when I worked in hotels and got free drinks, I did not drink again until I got out of law school. As a result of not drinking while going to law school, I became a very good student. In fact, I became a star student.

When I got my law degree, I was taken into a large Wall Street law firm. They hired me as sort of the resident immigrant. It was not a total loss, however, because instead of using foul language, I learned to react to things with "Oh really!" It became a sort of an all-purpose expression for me: "Oh really?" "Oh! *Really*!

My superiors at the law firm determined that I should be trained as a trial lawyer and sent me to the New York City courthouse to learn my trade. I wasn't up there too long before I discovered that the really bright lawyers were across the street in a saloon. So, I moved my whole operation into that saloon. There I learned to get drunk in a more civilized and genteel fashion.

About this time, it came time in my natural development that I be married. I met my current wife during the summer, while working as a bellhop at a hotel where she was a guest. Actually, bellhop to guest characterizes our relationship throughout our marriage. By the way, I always refer to her as my *current* wife because I find that it keeps her on her toes. She's been current for forty-five years.

My wife was from a different background than my own. Even though I drank a lot in those days, I was fully aware of the fact that her family had a buck or two. I will not burden you with the details of my wedding day, but I assure you that when my family from the South Bronx hit a Westchester country club, they set a few records.

My wife and I set up housekeeping and began to produce children with the regularity that is known only to the Roman Catholic. After the second child was born, I received a phone call from the Fordham University School of Law, asking me to come to see the dean. I went to see him and was appointed to the faculty.

Very few guys in my neighborhood became law professors. It frightened me to death. So, I decided to drink less for a while, until I got a handle on this job. After a few years had gone by, it turned out that I was a very competent law teacher and became a tenured professor. At that point, I thought it would be safe to go back to my usual manner of drinking. By that time, we had five kids, maybe more, and a very nice home. I was making good money.

If you had asked me how I was doing in those days, I would have told you that I was doing very well. As a matter of fact, I would have told you how well I was doing whether you asked me or not. My success was one of my favorite topics of conversation. The truth of the matter, however, was that at the age of thirty-four, I got drunk on a daily basis.

At this point, my wife began to talk in a very ugly fashion to me. She became very disloyal and said that there was something radically wrong with the way I drank. Well, since she was not an attorney and did not have the benefit of a legal education, I tried to explain things to her. One of the things I explained to her was the relativity of drinking. I explained that some people drink more than others and that on a relative scale, I was not such a big drinker. "As a matter of fact, I don't drink as much as my own mother," I explained. "Nobody drinks as much as your mother!" she answered.

My drinking drove my wife to distraction, and so she sought her physician's opinion, who as you might predict, was an obstetrician. He could find nothing the matter with her until she told him about me, in an act of gross disloyalty. He sent her home with a message. The message was that her doctor, the obstetrician, had diagnosed her husband, the law professor, as an alcoholic. To my knowledge, I am one of the few men who was referred to AA by a gynecologist.

Well, I was outraged and rose to defend myself with professional expertise, as was my custom. I took a very dim view of a physician who would diagnose a patient without ever having laid eyes upon him. "This type of shabby medical practice is all too common in our country today!" I exclaimed. Then I went into high gear and I asked my wife a question, to which she has not yet discovered an answer: "What kind of a man becomes an obstetrician in the first place?"

At this point, the conversation went downhill at a terrific rate and then it happened. I cannot explain how it happened, but in middle of all of my raving, I stopped and admitted for the first time ever that there had been many occasions upon which I had permitted myself to be over-served! That was as far as I cared to go at that time.

My wife, a woman of great resource, sprung into action. Three days later, I was a prisoner in a mental institution. Please understand that I did not surrender to anyone. They came and got me. Within moments of being there, I discovered a serious architectural deficiency in the building: There was no doorknob on my side of the door.

In addition to everything else, it was the occasion of my thirty-fifth birthday. I mentioned this to a man in a white coat walking in the hallway. I carefully explained to him that on this very day, under the Constitution of the United States of America, I was eligible for the office of President. He urged me not to plan my campaign yet, since there were two other presidents in residence, and he didn't want to tax security.

This was 1963, when there were no treatment centers for alcoholics, no twenty-eight day programs, and no alcoholism counselors. Today, virtually every jurisdiction has a Lawyer Assistance Program of some kind. Lawyers with any type of problem, whether it is drinking, drugs, depression, or anything else, can seek help under a shield of confidentiality. In my day, however, none of these services were available.

While I was participating in a monopoly therapy session with the other guys in the institution one day, someone told me that I had a visitor. This big, imposing looking guy, with a tie and a suit, announced that he was from AA and that the hospital had accused me of not cooperating. Can you imagine them accusing me of such, just because I would not go to occupational therapy to make moccasins?

Well, I reverted to my legal skills and started arguing with this man. He was very rude to me. Do you know what he said? You're not going to believe this. He said to me as follows: "Shut up!" I knew that they had neglected to tell him who I was, so I began to tell him. Again, he said, "shut up and sit down." Since he was a very imposing person, I sat down. Then, he began to tell me his story, much as I have been telling you mine.

Eventually, he asked me if I would like to go to meetings. "Meetings?" I asked, "What type of meetings?" He said that they would be meetings of a group known as Alcoholics Anonymous. "Oh really," I said. "Where are these meetings?" I asked. "They are outside of this institution," he answered. Once I heard that, I agreed to go with him.

He took me to his meetings and then made arrangements for me to go to meetings closer to home when I got out. That is how I started to go to AA meetings. I don't remember so much of that time because in those days, the medical community thought that the disease of alcoholism was caused by a deficiency of Valium. When one left an institution, one left with a jar full of these pills, which I popped into my mouth like candy. My instruction was that whenever I felt like a drink, I should have one of these pills. Well, since I felt like a drink every minute of the day, my head was buzzing all of the time.

My initial fantasies about AA were that I would become its president and get a plaque someday, but that didn't happen. I lasted 10 months and eventually got drunk again. I'm not going to take you through it all, except to say that I stayed drunk for a long stretch of time. It was, without question, the worst time of my life. Sometimes I wouldn't drink a week or a month, and come back to AA meetings. Then I would get drunk again for a long time.

Very bad things began to happen to me. I was asked to resign from my job as a tenured professor of law because I was a disgrace. I got into very serious personal, financial, and professional difficulty. I lost the affection of practically everyone that was around me, and spent the last several months of my drinking days sleeping in an automobile.

The worst part of it was that there seemed to be a terrible disintegration of my spirit. This was the spirit that once burned in me so brightly and was now extinguished. I knew that and couldn't do anything about it. I had been everywhere and nothing worked for me. I went through doctors, clergy, sanitariums, and I always ended up the same, drunk. I had come to think that it was not possible for someone like me to stop drinking. And then, one day, my time arrived.

I don't know too much about this, but it seems to me that there is a time for each of us. There is a line somewhere beyond which we're not permitted to go. It seems to me that there is a point somewhere below which we're not permitted to sink. There is a level of pain somewhere beyond which no human is required to endure.

For some, reaching the bottom may mean death. That is the way it was for my big brother. They called one day from a veterans hospital in Minneapolis to tell me that Billy had died of cirrhosis of the liver. He died in a way that many alcoholics do, without friends, without family, and a very long way from our home in the Bronx. For other people, this line to which I refer may be something trivial.

When I arrived at my bottom, it wasn't very different from so many other days. I was nervous, irritable and discontent, as usual. I had gotten into a law practice with some friends who barely tolerated me. Having gotten a big lump of money that day, the question arose as to whether I should go down to the bar in the lobby of our building and start drinking. Instead, I called the man who became my AA sponsor.

I called John because I could not live another day with that terror, that knowing that I was no good. I had this sense all of my life, and I don't know where it came from. All of my life, I had this feeling that I didn't belong. I just didn't fit in somehow.

Alcoholism would show up in my room around three in the morning, wake me up, and tell me that I was a bum. If it showed up at noon, I could argue with it, because I am good at arguing. But at three in the morning, this thing would tell me that I'm no good, that everyone is on to me, and that I'm a disgrace. I was a no good father, no good husband, and no good law teacher. It scared the life out of me, and that is what I was trying to get away from with my drinking.

I told all of this to my sponsor, and he gave me this look. These sponsors are like reptiles sometimes. They don't blink. They just look at you. Eventually, he said, “Well, if you don't drink and just go to the meetings, you'll be all right.”

I didn't want him to tell me that. I am a smart man and wanted to hear much more. I told him that he didn't understand the problem. The real problem, I told him, was that I was too good of a lawyer to work in this dump. He told me that I was very fortunate to be here at all. I explained that I didn't feel very well and he responded that this might be as good as I will ever feel. I asked him what he thought I should do, and he told me that I should hang on. “How do you hang on?” I asked. He said, “Let go.” It was like dealing with a Zen Buddhist.

I went on to explain to John that I needed more money because I had seven children. He told me that I would get a good job when I was ready. I asked when I would know that I was ready. He said that I would know it when I got a good job. I was getting no place with this man.

He took me to Grand Central Station and put me on a train. I lived in Larchmont, New York, a very upscale place, which was only appropriate for a lawyer of my stature, even though I was living in my car at the time. When I got off the train, standing on the platform was the man who delivered my mail, Al. He was the chairman of the local group.

Al said, “Get in the car.” I said to him, “With all due respect, I don't hang out with mailmen.” He told me that somebody had called him about me and that he would greatly appreciate it if I would just get into the car. I told Al that I was in trouble, and he told me that if I would just go to the meetings I would be okay. He took me to the meeting that night. That was November 24, 1965. When the meeting was over, Al told me that he would pick me up the next night at eight o’clock and that everything would be fine. I've never had a drink since.

I don't know how to explain it. My wife begged me to stop drinking, for her sake and the sake of our children. I said that I would, but I could not and I did not. My boss, the dean of my law school and godfather of one of my children, told me that I was a great teacher, but that the law school could not have a drunk around. I told him that I would stop for the sake of my career, but I could not and I did not. My physician, who really took a great interest in me, tried everything there was to get me to stop drinking. He tried to get me into long-term treatment, but I told him that I was taking care of it and did not need his help. I told him that I would stop drinking soon, but I didn't. I could not stop drinking for love or money. Then, out came a man from the post office and I never had a drink again. Do you think that they are teaching postal workers things that we don't know about?

Anyway, that is almost the end of my story. It has been close to thirty-five years since that day in November of 1965 and the world has turned over many times for me. In that time, I have come to a very basic conclusion that I would like to inflict upon you now: Alcoholism is not caused by alcohol. It seems to me that the problem is centered in the mind. The mind, of course, is the medical equivalent of the soul. I'm not a religious person and I don't go to church, but I am of the opinion that alcoholism is a disease of the spirit.

I don't think that it is a pure coincidence that the word "spirits" has several meanings, among which is a reference to distilled liquor. In 1960, Bill Wilson, one of the founders of AA, wrote to Carl Jung, the great Swiss psychiatrist, and asked him if he remembered a particular patient who later became very influential in Bill's life. Jung wrote back and said that he did indeed remember this patient, whom he could not help. The problem was, Jung explained, that this patient had separated himself from the "*whole*." Jung went on make a pun in Latin, "spiritus contra spiritum." The literal translation is "spirit against alcohol."

I came to this same conclusion years after I stopped drinking, and had the full opportunity to take the Twelve Steps of Alcoholics Anonymous. I will not go through them with you in detail, except to say that they include taking a "moral inventory," admitting your "defects of character," and making "direct amends" to people you have harmed. I did these things and discovered that rather than everyone else being at fault, as I had once known to be true, my difficulties came from within.

I found out that my problem was one of moral decay and a flawed character. It took guts to look into the mirror and work through these issues, but it was well worth it. Once I admitted these truths to myself and became willing to face up to them, good things just came pouring into my life. I won't bore you with what I have done with the rest of my life and the many successes I have had. Let's just say that today I consider myself a very lucky man.

In my drunken days, I hurt a lot of good people. Making amends to them was not easy, but the rewards were great. I once took fifteen thousand dollars from a colleague, as an advance for a book I was supposed to write with him over the summer, and never kept my end of the bargain. Years later, when I was finally in a position to give him back his money, this well-known New York lawyer would not take it. He wrote me a nice letter, basically stating that what was in the past was forgotten and that he wished me much luck in my endeavors to help other lawyers with similar problems.

When I think about that incident and the many other acts of kindness I have witnessed, I get choked up. Contrary to what I once thought, there is a great deal of goodness in people, if we just take the time to bring it out in them through our own acts of decency. Nothing bring tears to my eyes more than the time I was asked to come back to the Fordham School of Law and present my own daughter her law degree. In 1999, Fordham honored me with its first ever humanitarian award and announced that a portrait of me would shortly be hung on the Law School's wall!

It also occurs to me that much of what is wrong with our profession goes back to a deterioration of the spirit. The alcoholic lawyer is just one type of symptomatic casualty of this condition. As a result of a devolution of their spirits, some lawyers get depressed, while others suffer from heart and stomach problems. The most common symptom of the problem is evidenced by the number of lawyers who are consumed with anger and act uncivilly toward each other, thinking that money is the ultimate measure of their success. Such lawyers suffer from an extinguished inner spirit that once lit their way. It seems to me that the solution is a simple one, if we only have the courage to invoke it.

Every calling is great when greatly pursued. But what other gives such scope to realize the spontaneous energy of one's soul? In what other does one plunge so deep in the stream of life - so share its passions, its battles, its despair, its triumphs, both as witness and actor?

But that is not all. What a subject is this in which we are united - this abstraction called the Law, wherein, as in a magic mirror, we see reflected, not only our own lives, but the lives of all men that have been! When I think on this majestic scene, my eyes dazzle.

Oliver Wendell Holmes

Alienation Of Affections

Amiram Elwork*

It was a horrifying nightmare, filled with paralytic fear and a crushing sensation in his chest. Jack envisioned himself experiencing a heart attack, being rushed to a hospital, lying in an intensive care unit, and being hooked up to a monitor. A doctor was telling family members that it was now up to Jack's will to live. "Letting go would solve all of my problems!" he observed himself thinking in his dream. The right decision seemed obvious. Just as he was ready to give up on life, however, he awoke in a sweat, repeatedly crying out loud, "No, damn it! No!"

As Jack became fully conscious of himself, he realized that Emily was holding him tightly and saying softly, "It's okay, it's okay, Jack. It's just a bad dream." He felt himself sweating and shivering at the same time, much like he did many years ago

---

* Dr. Amiram Elwork is the Director of the Law-Psychology (J.D.-Psy.D.) Graduate Program at Widener University, near Philadelphia, and he has a consulting practice that serves the legal community. He has written numerous articles and several books on "psycholegal" issues, including "Making Jury Instructions Understandable" and "Stress Management for Lawyers."

after a drunken stupor. This highly respected lawyer, who many feared to face in the courtroom, was reduced to a curled up fetal position. Jack's body was much more massive than Emily's, and his graying hair and unshaven, leathery face made him look much older than she. Although there was something visually incongruous about it, Emily was providing Jack with what he desperately needed right now, the physical warmth of a motherly body.

"What's happening to me?" Jack asked himself in desperation. His nightmare seemed so real. What did it all mean? Was it an expression of his fear of death or of a wish to die? Something in him suggested that it was the latter possibility, which was the more distressing of the two. "Why would I want to give up and die?" he asked himself again and again.

For what seemed like a long time, though it was only for a few minutes, Emily held Jack in her arms and calmed him down with soft whispers, much like a mother does with a crying infant. The mothering role was a very natural one for Emily, but not in this context. She had always depended on Jack to be strong and it frightened her to see him like this. She knew, however, that this was not the time to be dependent. Emily had to take charge, and she did just that.

When he regained his composure, Jack recounted his dream for Emily. "What do you think it means?" he said. "Am I having a nervous breakdown?"

"I don't know, but I have a suspicion," Emily said.

"What? Tell me!" Jack said anxiously.

Generally, when it came to discussing personal issues, Jack was not a good listener. He had a hard time standing or sitting still and attending to such conversations. At the office and with his clients, however, he was highly attentive and never missed a detail. There was simply no time in his life for having soft-headed personal discourse and it made him feel uneasy. This conversation was different, however. And so, he asked again, "Tell me. What do you think is wrong?"

"Lately, I have been feeling that you are becoming more and more distant," Emily said softly. "You hardly ever express your affection like you used to do or accept it from others."

Emily's words caused Jack's eyes to get teary. Intuitively, he knew she was right on the mark. For a moment, however, his analytical side chose to divert attention from the meanings of her words, and instead to admire how succinct and precise Emily was. Concise and exact communication is something he tried to instill in his associates at the office, but somehow never expected of his wife. Although she had surprised him with this ability on a number of occasions, he preferred not to credit her with it.

Emily was definitely a feeler more than she was a thinker. It was the thing that had kept him from fully respecting her and allowed him to feel somewhat superior to her - something he needed to feel, no doubt. Now, he was looking up to *her* for clarity and guidance.

"What do you mean, Emily?" Jack asked quietly.

"You've been acting lately as though you just don't have time for anybody," Emily went on. "Even the dog has reacted to it. The next time anyone walks in to the house, notice how Brandeis comes running with his tail wagging. When you walk in, he barely lifts his head anymore. Sometimes I wonder if you still love your family. Will there be anything left to our relationship after the kids are gone?"

"Please don't say that," Jack responded with a crackle in his voice. They embraced each other tightly and continued their conversation for a while longer, until each fell asleep again.

Upon awakening, the experiences of the previous night seemed surreal. Luckily, it was Sunday, and Jack had some time to recuperate from his emotional upheaval. In the comfort of his warm bed, with his eyes half shut so as to not let on that he was awake, he watched Emily dress and groom herself. She was also forty nine years old, but her petite size and smooth skin made her look younger than her years. There was still a glow in her attractive oval face, which projected a certain happiness that is born of good will.

"How beautiful she is," he thought to himself but seldom told her. Saying "I love you," was a complicated matter for Jack. The meaning of those words couldn't just be felt. They had to be defined, qualified and clarified. Most of the time, it was easier to say nothing.

At moments like this he also felt guilty about being critical of her at times, especially since she tended to take it so personally. For him, arguments were nothing more than a tool of discovery. For her, they were signs of disharmony and very threatening. As he watched this gentle lady brush her light brown hair in the morning light, he considered himself to be her protector, in charge of making sure that her spirit wouldn't get wounded. Such musings evoked confusing and inexpressible emotions in him.

While he lingered in his bed, Jack began to think about his problem with the same type of systematic logic that he applied to legal issues. "I don't have any time to waste," he thought to himself as he began to plan his strategy.

Although Jack was not a religious man, he chose to consider his dreadful dream to be a warning of things to come unless he dramatically changed his life. The emotional experience was so intense, filled with so much fear, that he might as well have had a real heart attack and been lying in a real hospital.

The words "foxhole religion" repeatedly popped into Jack's mind. It was a phrase used to describe how quickly soldiers become "believers" when their survival is on the line. Jack wondered if his reaction was genuine or whether it would wane with the passage of time. In reflecting on all that had occurred, however, it was clear to him that something was seriously wrong and that he needed to correct it.

When Jack finally moved his weary body downstairs to the kitchen, his two teenage children were already out of the house, but Emily was still there. She greeted him with a smile and asked how he was feeling. "Tired," he said, experiencing a tinge of embarrassment about the extent to which he had revealed himself last night, albeit to his best friend. His usual self would have filled a bowl of cereal and begun reading the paper in isolation. Intuitively, he knew that now was not the time to do that.

Brandeis, who was sunbathing by the kitchen window, had not acknowledged Jack's entrance with even a wag of his tail, just as Emily had noticed. Jack reflected on the fact that dogs are very uncomplicated creatures. In fact, Brandeis' relationship with him contained all of the elements of what was wrong in simple, but elegant terms.

Jack had been the one who had brought the dog home for the kids some ten years earlier and named him after an admired Supreme Court Justice. At one time, he and the dog had a very close relationship. Now, it was nonexistent. It was as if Brandeis had said to himself, "Since I've become invisible to you, there is no need to make believe that you exist either."

Jack called the dog several times, but Brandeis did not budge. It was going to take more than a simple desire on Jack's part to repair his relationships. Jack realized that he could not expect everyone else to wipe the plate clean, just because he had pronounced his desire to change. It would take extended action on his part before others would trust his intent again.

Jack got up from his chair, walked over to Brandeis and started petting him. Now, Brandeis' tail began to wag ever so slightly. Eventually, he even lifted his head and licked Jack's hand.

"Will it be this easy with you and the kids?" Jack asked Emily.

"I don't think so," Emily replied.

"How about you, puppy? How long will it take you to care if I come or go again?" Jack asked rhetorically.

Brandeis turned over on his back, as if to say, "Scratch my belly, and then we'll talk." Jack realized that he hadn't played with the dog in a very long time and remembered that it was enjoyable.

Over their morning coffee, Jack and Emily continued their conversation of last night. "You're right Emily," Jack said. "I have been feeling increasingly numb for the last few years, but I don't know why."

"What keeps flashing in my head is when we first met at Cornell," Emily replied. "Even then you took things a little too seriously, but still, you knew how to have fun. You sang along with the car radio and joked with people you met in the street. The guy I married dreamed of making a contribution to society someday. It wasn't all about money. Do you remember?" Emily asked Jack rhetorically.

"That passion, Jack, you just don't have it anymore," Emily continued. "I think it started when you went to law school at Penn, and I got busy at my teaching job and later with the kids, but I don't really know exactly what happened. Maybe you should talk to someone."

Jack and Emily spent the afternoon together, working in the yard and going to see a movie. Emily talked Jack into one of those limited-distribution motion pictures that play only at the “artsy” theaters. The movie sounded like it was going to be sentimental, which appealed to Emily but not to Jack. Given what had just transpired, though, he had no choice but to appease her.

Deep down Jack knew that people were right about Emily. She had to be an “angel” to be able to live with him, and he was lucky to be married to her. He was one of those aggressive lawyers, whose dealings with the darker sides of human nature had turned him into a cynic. If you could overlook his insensitivity, Jack could be a good friend, but it took work to relate to him.

In contrast, Emily was easy to like. Unlike him, she was gracious and always knew the right things to say, even at times when there was nothing to say. If it wasn’t for Emily, Jack suspected, he would have no friends. In addition, she was one of the few people on earth who truly loved him. Although it would not be readily apparent to anyone who simply focused on Jack’s many successes at law, he needed Emily and was very dependent on her.

When the lights dimmed at the theater, Jack figured he could just use the time to ponder his life. To his own surprise, however, the soundtrack at the beginning of the movie, featuring Janis Joplin singing "Summertime," stirred something in him. He remembered seeing her in concert over thirty years earlier at a rock festival, while in college. As the movie progressed, he found himself emotionally aroused by several of the other old songs being played in the background. Eventually, a few unexplainable tears rolled down his cheeks.

As a litigator, he had gotten very adept at suppressing his emotions. When you are standing in front of a judge and jury, you can't afford to let any type of negative affect pull you down. All those years of practice were being called on to help him get through this movie. "You don't need a degree in psychology to figure this out," he thought to himself. After all, he was turning fifty soon and sentimental reminiscences were to be expected. This was sort of like a man's version of hot flashes he joked to himself. "It's nothing. It will pass," he concluded.

Later that evening, the family went out to dinner. Jack was uncharacteristically subdued and pensive. He observed himself looking at his kids and wife through the lenses of a person who had been away for a long time. A part of him felt sad for having missed seeing them grow the last few years and for being too busy or distant to truly share in their most important experiences. Another part of him felt exceptionally fortunate and joyful to be with them in the present. "Is this what love is?" Jack asked himself.

After a restless night of internal confusion, the next day Jack went to work and found himself marching down to see "Old Ben," one of the original founders of the firm. Ben was eighty-one years old and still insisted on coming in twice a week, on Mondays and Thursdays. At one time he had been a great lawyer, but now was happy to help out in any way he could - even do library research if that was needed.

Ben came in because he loved the law and the law firm he helped to create; he enjoyed spending his time in such surroundings. It was also a form of exercise for him. Ben was of the opinion that, much like his muscles, his brain needed a certain level of regularly scheduled problem-solving activity to maintain its vitality. Indeed, while his eye sight and hearing were beginning to fail him and he walked with a slight limp, all who would take the time to speak to Ben were amazed at his mental acuity.

Many of the partners had a love-hate relationship with Ben. In some ways they revered him and found his presence in the firm, and at all partners' meetings and social occasions, to be very comforting. At other times, they found his presence to be frustrating. Ben saw himself as the preserver of old values. He didn't speak much at partners' meetings, but when he did speak, his opinions carried great authority. On a number of occasions, his mere objection to some proposed changes at the firm was enough to block them. Some partners secretly waited for a time when he would no longer be a member of the firm and they would no longer have to pay deference to him.

Ben also had a reputation for being a great mentor. Associates loved to ask him questions. Not only did he have a wealth of knowledge that one can only get through experience, but he had the patience to respond to their questions as if he had all the time in the world. On occasion, senior partners asked for his counsel as well, especially when they were involved in highly unusual cases and wondered if he had ever encountered a similar situation.

Jack had never sought Ben's advice on a personal matter before, but he couldn't think of anyone more appropriate with whom to discuss such problems. Ben greeted Jack warmly that morning, and agreed to meet him for lunch that afternoon. Jack was surprised to hear that most of Ben's day was completely booked.

At lunch that day, Jack began to tell Ben some of what had happened that past weekend at home and asked him if he had ever experienced such an episode.

"I've never had a dream like that, but I've experienced the alienation that your wife described," Ben responded. "Unfortunately, I've watched more and more lawyers become that way in recent years."

"What do you think I should do?" Jack asked.

"Well, of course, each of us is different, but I can tell you how I dealt with it," Ben replied. "One of the things that I've learned over the years, Jack, is that life is really quite simple. It's nowhere near as complicated as we like to pretend so that we can have an excuse for not solving our problems."

"Uh huh," Jack nodded, waiting for Ben to get into the core of his argument.

"I came to realize that the best lawyers I have ever known, all had three main qualities," Ben continued. "They were all highly competent, had unshakable integrity, and truly cared – about their families, their colleagues, their clients, and their community. It sounds to me that you've been neglecting that third component. I've learned the hard way that caring about things is at least as important as being competent and ethical in life."

"Uh huh," Jack muttered politely, not exactly seeing how this was going to help him.

"Think about it from a client's perspective," Ben continued. "What do most clients want in their lawyers, or doctors or any professionals on whom they depend for important matters? Would you ever want an incompetent surgeon to operate on you? Of course not. That would be too risky. Similarly, why wouldn't you want a surgeon who lacked integrity to operate on you, even if he was competent?"

"I guess, I would wonder if the operation was necessary to begin with, or whether I was just helping the surgeon pay for his summer home," Jack responded.

"Right!" Ben exclaimed. "Now, answer this question. What difference would it make if the surgeon cared in the least about you? As long as the surgeon is competent and has high integrity, wouldn't the operation go equally as well, regardless of whether he cared?"

"Well, let's see," said Jack. "Most people would like to think that their surgeons care about them, but I am not sure that it does make a difference – other than feeling good about your surgeon."

"That's where you are wrong, Jack," Ben said with a smile. "Suppose something terrible goes wrong on the operating table, you are literally dying, and the operating team needs to send shock through your heart to get it pumping again or use other emergency measures to bring you back to life. After a while, the surgeon has the option to declare you officially dead or to keep trying. Now, would you want a caring surgeon or a non-caring one?"

"I see your point," Jack said.

"A caring surgeon is also more likely to maintain his competence level and to not let circumstances dissuade him from his integrity," Ben continued as if he had not heard Jack's response.

"I see your point, Ben, but I still don't understand how this relates to my situation," Jack said politely.

"You asked me before how I think you should deal with your feelings of alienation. The first thing you need to do is understand how you got to where you are. My hunch is that your situation has come about because you have mistakenly placed too much importance on competence and integrity, without recognizing that there is a critical third component, without which the first two cannot survive," Ben said.

"I think I understand," Jack pronounced in a confused manner.

"You see, Jack," Ben went on, "yours is a problem many lawyers experience today. It wasn't nearly so bad in my day, but it's always been a hazard of our profession. I think that our law professors are partly responsible. Their idea of teaching you to think like a lawyer is to get you to rely solely on your intellect, as if that is a wise thing to do. They try to strip you of your emotions – your caring side, as if that is a good thing to do. The net effect, I've realized, is to make it possible for you to squelch your conscience. That's how you stop caring, first about little things and eventually about everything and everyone, including life itself. Now do you understand?"

"Yes, I think I do, Ben," Jack responded with a slight break in his voice. He had not been prepared for the depth with which Ben had obviously thought this through. "How did you come to realize all of this?" Jack asked.

"My youngest son died in an automobile accident at the age of 17," Ben replied. "I was a little older than you, then, but not by much. When it first happened, I felt totally numb. People told me that my initial reaction was to be expected and that soon enough I would feel grief. As time went on, I found that I was still numb and not experiencing real grief. You see, Jack, some of us achieve numbness of mind through alcohol or drugs, but I had enough self-control to do it all by myself. Eventually, I came to realize that I had lost my capacity to love my son or anyone," Ben recalled with tears in his eyes. "In fact, I came to realize that I had hardly known my son. My own flesh and blood, came and went, and I barely knew him. I was too busy with work. After my son's death, I began to search for a different way."

Jack felt fortunate to have had the benefit of Ben's wisdom and regretful that he hadn't sought it out before. Mostly, Jack felt a mixture of fear and guilt about possibly not being up to the task of changing, but he was determined to try.

It took several weeks of relating to Brandeis before he began to wag his tail upon seeing Jack walk into the house. The rest of the family took much longer to come around. For a very long time Jack worked on re-igniting his love for them. He learned to allow his body to feel true gratitude at seeing and being with his family again. Out of such feelings, his loving behaviors steadily became more natural and genuine. Only then, did his children and wife respond in kind.

Although it was awkward at first, Jack forced himself to change at the office as well. First, he worked on his relationship with his secretary, Cindy. With Emily's coaching, Jack began to use words like "please" and "thank you" much more often and to take real interest in her life through engaging conversations. Soon he found out that Cindy was boasting about her great boss and noticed that her productivity and dedication improved greatly.

For similar reasons, Jack noticed improvements in his relationships with associates. He also learned that it was best to let go of a few of his clients, especially those whose personalities were exceedingly unpleasant. On the other hand, he found that once he began to care about his clients, they responded in kind and were much more loyal to him than before.

Jack's relationships with his partners went through a difficult transformation. His rediscovered personal values clashed with some of his partners' values. He became interested in pursuing greater satisfaction at practicing law and achieving more balance in his life outside of the office. Some of his partners were where he had been, focusing primarily on professional success and viewing numbers like billable hours as the way to measure that success.

Several of Jack's partners learned to admire the "new" Jack and even looked up to him for changing his ways. Others were critical of his seemingly reduced level of dedication to law. In truth, he was no longer willing to sacrifice so much of his personal life for the firm. Eventually he had to accept a downward adjustment in his annual income. He was still making an excellent living, though, and was able to justify his lower income every time he looked into his children's and Emily's eyes.

Begrudgingly, some of the critical partners had to admit that in several ways Jack had become an even more valuable member of the firm than before. He was attracting new clients with much greater ease than others in the firm. In addition, he became a good mentor and learned to leverage his talents through more effective delegation.

Still, Jack had to endure a combination of some criticism and jealousy, and at times considered either leaving the firm for another or starting one of his own. He found himself seated next to "Old Ben" more often than before at partners' meetings and agreeing with him on many important issues. Eventually, after Ben passed away, Jack and several other partners who had been touched by the old man's wisdom took over his role, and tried to make sure that the firm did not lose sight of that third component - caring. The topic seemed to come up whenever there was a discussion about running the firm like a "business."

It took Jack a number of years to undergo his metamorphosis. There were many obstacles to overcome, and he often felt as though he was stumbling through the night. Nevertheless, whenever he reflected on how alienated from everyone and everything he once felt, he smiled to himself and repeatedly came to the same conclusion: The changes he had made were the most difficult accomplishments of his life, but they were well worth it!

"I don't say embrace trouble...... But I do say meet it as a friend, for you'll see a lot of it and had better be on speaking terms with it."

Oliver Wendell Holmes

Life Is Too Short

Carmen V. Roberto*

Besides being one of the funniest people I know, my father is an extremely wise man. He taught me two very important things:

1. Do not tell people everything you know.
2.

He explained that especially when you don't know much, which is often the case with me, the second important thing is superfluous.

Because of my dad, my two brothers and I grew up in a household full of the kind of laughter that made your belly ache. We learned that humor could set people at ease, tone down a tense situation, accentuate an important point, and generally help you through tough times. I only wish that more of my legal colleagues could learn that lesson.

Stress is a lawyer's constant companion. It will creep out in the middle of an ill-fated cross-

---

* Carmen V. Roberto is a practicing attorney in Akron, Ohio, with the firm of Vasko, Roberto & Evans Co., L.P.A. A former president of the Akron Bar Association, he has sat on the boards of several charitable, community and public agencies.

examination, sneak up on you during a bad-news phone call, and wallop you on the head when an unexpected verdict is read. Among the things that can significantly help you get through most situations is a healthy sense of humor. With over twenty-five years of experience in thousands of court proceedings, humor was the thing that bailed me out on numerous occasions. Here are some examples:

Once upon a time I was a young, energetic and terrified prosecutor, trying one of my first cases. A young boy had been hit by a car so hard that it knocked him out of his boots and sent him flying some thirty-seven feet. Somehow, he survived. During my closing argument at this hit and run prosecution, I showed the jury just how far the young boy had flown. I did this by pacing off thirty-seven steps all the way out of the courtroom and into the hallway, where I was no longer visible. Everyone began laughing. After a few minutes, I walked back in and said: "Ladies and gentlemen, this defendant knocked that poor boy out of sight also. I was in the hall for three minutes. He lay there bleeding for three hours." Then I sat down. The jury's verdict was "guilty."

Another of my favorite war stories involved a judge who was known to be cantankerous, but who had a great sense of humor. He hated being reversed so he seldom ruled against defense lawyers on objections. In one particularly testy trial in which I was the prosecutor, he overruled me so frequently I began keeping a checklist. After some fifteen consecutive unfavorable rulings, I said "Bingo" and asked to approach the bench. I could see the jurors smiling. They usually know what's going on, even though we like to think they don't.

With a huge smile, I told the judge that he had overruled me fifteen times in a row.

He said, "So what?"

I replied, "I'm having trouble believing that I'm that stupid, Your Honor. And, I'm really wrestling with the notion that you could be that smart."

He laughed and nodded his head. The jurors smiled as well. That eased the tension and cured the problem. The evidence did not change, but the atmosphere did and a difficult trial became far less stressful for everyone. This time, the jury's verdict was "not guilty."

On yet another occasion, I had the privilege of trying a case before a "hizzoner" jurist who was known to push things along in a no-nonsense way. After a three-day trial involving hundreds of documents, he asked if twenty minutes would be enough for closing arguments.

"Your Honor, I'll need more time than that to properly praise the Court for the manner in which you conducted the trial," I quipped. With a smile, his response was, "Take all the time you need."

Let me end with a final true story that isn't meant to be funny. When Lincoln's funeral train passed through Cleveland, a young girl ran from the crowd and placed a single flower on the casket. Her name is lost to the ages. But from that simple act of kindness arose the tradition in our culture of giving flowers at funerals. It goes to show how far a nice gesture can ripple out.

I believe that if you recognize that everyone in our business is under constant stress and if you relieve a smidgen of it through humor, you will find that even your incorrigible colleagues will treat you better. If you have no comedic talent whatsoever, at least try to smile more often. I assure you that it will make your voice sound happy and your conversations more pleasant. So, did you hear the one about the lawyer who outwitted the devil?

Practicing Law While Living Within The Wheel Of Life

Samuel P. Guyton*

The lives of many lawyers are dangerously out of balance today. Even when they recognize this, they are bewildered as to what to do. Many believe that an unbalanced life is an inevitable and unavoidable consequence of practicing law. However, I am convinced this is not necessarily so because I remember a time when lawyers' lives were more balanced. In addition, I have lost my own balance many times and know that this stressful and debilitating condition *is* avoidable. The most effective way for me to convince you of this issue is to tell you my story and what I have learned along the way.

---

* Samuel P. Guyton , now retired, was formerly a partner with the firm of Holland & Hart in Denver, and is presently President of the Holland & Hart Foundation, a volunteer charitable and educational organization. Mr. Guyton also volunteers his time in several other community service organizations. He has been active in the American and Colorado Bar Associations, and has taken leadership roles in the American College of Tax Counsel, the American Tax Policy Institute, and the Tax Section of the Colorado Bar Association.

One of the lawyers who inspired me to consider law as a career was my own grandfather, whose picture hangs on my office wall. He loved the law and delighted in serving others. Occasionally, his family members lodged complaints that he didn't charge enough for his legal work. Nevertheless, they were proud of the fact that through the years, first as a lawyer and later as a judge, he helped countless persons.

While his work was a significant part of his life, my grandfather never lost sight of the importance of a full life. He was a thoughtful and articulate man who had an endearing jocund nature and laughed at his own stories harder and longer than anyone else. One of the stories he told was about the time he was driving to hear a case at an out of town court, and stopped to wet a line at an inviting fishing hole. His court reporter became extremely nervous and told him they would be late for court, to which my grandfather replied with the customary twinkle in his eye: "Well, they can't start without us, can they?"

As a young boy, I observed with considerable awe the place of honor many other lawyers held in society. In the community where I grew up, lawyers were esteemed leaders in civic, religious, governmental, cultural and educational organizations. They were highly regarded for their wisdom, understanding and sense of justice. They were concerned about the welfare of the poor, interested in the well-being of individuals and the greater good of the community, and adept at solving problems.

The lawyers I knew spent time with their families and friends, took time for their own interests and helped others. They were seldom too busy to listen to others or to give friendly and helpful advice, when asked. Some of them were my teachers and mentors in various organizations.

Without a doubt, the lawyers I knew made a positive difference in the lives of others and were at the forefront of creating a just and humane society. By finding purpose in all of their activities, and by having balance in their lives, they taught what they lived. Naturally, I wanted to be just like them. And so, I went to law school.

The Beginnings Of Imbalance

In my early years after law school, the lawyers in my firm possessed many of the same commendable traits I had seen and admired in my grandfather and the other attorneys in my home community. The older lawyers in my firm were true mentors. They took ample time to explain how to handle complex legal transactions and how to treat clients and others with respect. They were never too busy to spend time talking about different aspects of the law or about their outside interests. They also took a personal interest in me and my family, and in our activities outside of the firm.

Still, the "times they were a changing." One of the founders of my firm told me that the practice of law had to change. Lawyers had to become more mindful of running their practices in a business-like manner. Eventually, increasing competition and costs, and a desire to become more efficient and profitable resulted in a louder drumbeat to work harder and harder.

This had a dramatic and personal impact on me. I felt I had to take every work assignment from older lawyers. As an individual who wanted to please, I was reluctant to ever say "no" or " I am too busy to help with that project." Outwardly, I projected a pleasant demeanor and an attitude that said: "I can do anything you ask me to do." Even when I started to generate clients of my own for the firm, I continued to take on the same load assigned to me by senior lawyers. I worked long hours each day and most weekends.

I tried valiantly to save some time for my family and did so periodically, but the principal focus of my life was my work. In fact, I felt guilty whenever I wasn't working. To illustrate how imbalanced my life had become, I chose to be at the office on the weekend when my wife was in the hospital giving birth to our third child. The thought of that insensitivity still pains me.

My body, functioning as a feedback and early warning system, gave the knell that I was in big trouble by signaling, through a severe physical impairment, that I was in enormous difficulty. Close to a physical and mental breakdown, I was put under a doctor's care. I had to "feel the pain to make a change." At the same time, I was fearful of revealing my stress and suffering to anyone.

Luckily, one observant older lawyer recognized what was happening and threw out a lifeline that saved me. This dear friend walked into my office one day and told me to leave and not come back for at least two weeks. I balked and denied that anything was wrong with me. I looked at all the work piled high on my desk and declared that there was no way I could go away. He would not hear one word of my protestation. I was basically kicked out of the office and told to rest and recover, which I did with the assistance of my understanding wife.

In the nick of time, this intervention by a sympathetic mentor created space for a small degree of harmony to enter my life. This could not have happened on my own volition. I needed a strong signal to wake and shake me out of my self-imposed stupor. Outside assistance was required for me to see that I was totally out of balance and to help me find a modicum of equilibrium.

External Rescues

After a forced leave of absence from my firm, I was never again in such a desperate and seemingly helpless condition. I was careful to monitor the level of my work load and to decline taking on more than I could handle. Nevertheless, the practice still occupied most of my time and attention - physically, mentally, and emotionally.

I was spending more time with my family, but even when I was physically with my family, my mind would be fixed on some work related issue. When I was with my family mentally, I felt compelled to act like a lawyer, which meant winning every argument. On one occasion, I argued with everyone in my family about the actual time that the moon was full. The encyclopedia supported my family's position, but even that did not deter me. It seemed I always had to be right. As with my previous encounter with imbalance, help came from an outside source.

The siren's grasp and allure placed on me by my practice was thankfully broken by the bold intervention of my wife. She confronted me and told me with great frankness how I was injuring her and others by my preoccupation with work. I was stunned when she told me this and at first argued vociferously that she was wrong. Unyieldingly, I insisted that my love and care for her and our children were the principal reasons I was working so hard. I felt wounded that she thought otherwise. She tried to make me understand that all she and our children wanted was more of my time and attention. When she requested that I get some professional counseling, I was initially resistant. Then, I thought to myself that perhaps this would make her feel better and show my love for her.

Fortunately, my firm had established an Employees Assistance Program (EAP) that provided timely and effective counseling. With guidance, I was able to see the totality of my being and realize how my practice had unknowingly subsumed other essential parts of my life. For the first time since I was a child, I saw the importance of reserving some time for myself and my personal development.

I discovered that I had lived by the erroneous, but what I thought was the immutable principle: "Work before play." The problem with this rule was that there was a never ending stream of work, no matter how long and hard I slaved away. Even though not defining myself by my work continued to be a challenge, I began to be able to look more objectively at my life and recognize if I was out of equilibrium. This allowed me to restore some semblance of balance.

Like many attorneys I know, I felt I was always expected to say that I was buried by work. This showed that I was not a laggard and helped me commiserate with my colleagues about the mutual and seemingly helpless state of being overburdened. I attempted to move a step beyond this by acknowledging to others the lack of harmony in my life while affirming that I was attempting to address it as best I could. Another tactic I employed was to tell the firm's compensation committee that the amount awarded me was more than I deserved (which it truly was). I did this in the belief that if my compensation were reduced I would not feel compelled to work so hard. This was not very successful as my compensation was not changed.

Several programs established by my firm helped me and other lawyers find some equilibrium in our lives. One was a sabbatical program started in the early 1970s. This program taught me I was dispensable. Others could handle my clients when I was not in the office for several months and my clients were still there when I returned. This helped me get some perspective on my life and ponder what values were most important to me.

Another beneficial program was the previously mentioned Employees Assistance Program. I became a member and later chairman of a firm committee designated to deal with the personal and professional problems of partners by providing a safe place to hear and assist them with their concerns. The addictive and harmful effects of alcoholism, drugs and workaholism I saw emerging in our profession, also affected some of my colleagues. With professional assistance at times, the committee and I attempted to assist our fellow partners. I discovered that by assisting others I became more able to see ways in which I could bring greater harmony into my own life.

Other helpful programs implemented by my firm were frequent intra-office communications and seminars on subjects such as stopping smoking, weight control and preparing for retirement and other life transactions. A liberal maternity-paternity policy, an innovative and extended health program with annual physicals, flexible work schedules, firm wide social and recreational activities, and the availability of mountain condominiums for attorneys were indicators of the firm's recognition that it was important for people to have a life other than work. Highlighting my firm's recognition of the importance of balance was the adoption of a Statement of Principles to support the purpose of the firm, which was "to provide quality legal services which are timely and suited to our clients' requirements, and to do so on a profitable basis in a pleasant and satisfying work environment."

Internal Transformations

As I found more and more equilibrium, I began to recognize the almost total cerebral nature of my law practice and the omission of other essential ingredients in my life. I also realized that I was a "time slave." My worth and value were being measured in six minute segments at the office, and I was translating this into other spheres of my life as well. Gradually, I began to realize that time is not real, but that life is real. Time is only a tool I use in my life. The challenge for me was not to make a measuring tool the sine qua non of life. This took a number of deeply internal transformations.

A core concept that was of great help to me in my internal struggle for balance is a Native American belief in the Wheel or Circle of Life. As viewed by this tradition, our lives are like moving wheels, and the spokes represent our mind, body, spirit and natural environment. The manner in which these interact with all areas of our lives make up the wheel. How we choose to live our lives is reflected in the dimensions and spacing of the various spokes. The warp of the moving wheel reveals our state of harmony. There is no absolute and perpetual state of complete and total equilibrium. As the wheel turns, mirroring how we have chosen to live our lives, sometimes there is more balance, and at times there is less balance.

A Native American friend, who is also a lawyer, told me that every individual has the capacity for becoming more balanced on the Wheel of Life. Some indices of improved equilibrium are: having time for others, listening to them with full attention, seeing the value and worth of every individual, refusing to judge people simply by our own standards, not comparing ourselves with others, not trying to control others, and helping those who have fallen off the wheel get back on it.

My friend instructed me that living a life of equability on the wheel does not mean the absence of conflict, disappointments, challenges, pain or even debilitating stress. What it means is being aware of our state of balance or imbalance and then making constructive and creative choices to achieve the desired state. This was the key for me: being conscious of when I was on or off the wheel and taking corrective action to adjust my spokes.

With the inestimable support of my family and my firm, I was able to do this by increasing the dimensions of the mind, body, spirit and natural environment spokes on my Wheel of Life and finding some space between them in the work, rest and play areas of my life. Still, work claimed the most dominant space and received the most attention. Many times I continued to feel like a rat in a maze. During these times, if my life had been put to music, it would not have reflected euphony, but rather a cacophony of dissonance. In fact, one helpful technique I used in monitoring my state of balance was to ask what would my life sound like if I put it to music. This did not quell the raucous sounds, but it did make me alert to my state as it was a clarion call to try and do something to lessen the deafening roar.

I discovered that asking myself certain questions revealed where I was on the Wheel of Life: What is important in my life? How much time and energy am I devoting to what I value most in my life? Does my appointment calendar reveal what I treasure and think is most essential in my life? If my life ended today, would I view it as being fulfilled by what I accomplished as a lawyer, a husband, a father, a friend and a human being?

Another aid I occasionally used in evaluating the degree of equilibrium in my life was to ask a family member or an understanding colleague questions about what I was doing, and to determine from their answers if my life needed more harmony. My challenge was to bring some measure of change in my life without causing my clients and fellow lawyers to complain. This juggling act was never easy and often frustrating, but at the same time it was essential for my overall well-being. At times, I would observe that I was living life mechanistically and without the joy I desired, but work obligations were such that I was perplexed about how to change direction. Over time, a formula slowly emerged that assisted me in bringing more equilibrium into my life. This formula was characterized by three distinct words: *silencing, self and service.*

Silencing was a grounding principle for me. It involved reminding myself to create a large sign in my mind with the letters S T O P. When I did that, I had to come to a halt and slow down my fast beating heart, my run away emotions and my buzzing mind. Putting on breaks at a breakneck speed is not easy and sometimes I wore out the brake linings trying to do so. With time and practice, I calmed myself by taking a few deep and measured breaths and by saying: “I need a break.”

I was best able to take breaks by closeting myself in my office. Sometimes, I just imagined I was going to a place of quiet and peace or used meditation techniques. These were restorative. Each day I attempted to schedule a few moments for just silencing. When I found myself saying I didn’t have time for these silencing periods, this was a signal to be sure and include them.

I even developed a list of those things which most stressed me and then let these things be a reminder to me of the need for quieting myself, even if it was only for a very brief moment. For instance, the constantly ringing telephone was one of the biggest stressors in my professional life. So, every time the phone would ring, I would treat this as a signal for me to center and calm myself. I would never answer the phone until at least the third ring as I repeated to myself: “This ringing is a signal to calm myself.” I also got into the habit of taking brief pauses between projects.

In a way, my silencing periods were forms of fasting from work. Yet, they gave me the ability and energy to be more effective and productive in my practice. Additionally, they made me more conscious of the times when I was proceeding on automatic drive. I used these periods to consider how I might live out and foster my life's purposes, including nourishing the choices that supported such purposes and eliminating or reducing those activities that detracted me.

Being a lover of the out-of-doors, I delighted in being by myself while hiking, fishing, skiing or climbing. Echoing loudly in my mind, however, was the familiar refrain: "No play until the work is all done." The problem was that work was never done. As I became more balanced, I began to comprehend that my greatest asset to my clients was my ability to help them solve their problems creatively. How could I be creative if I had no time set aside for recharging my own batteries - taking time for *self*? I came to understand the necessity of scheduling such time on my calendar. Taking time for myself was very difficult, but with the help of my wife I was able to get past my feelings of guilt when I did so.

The third step to more harmony in my life was that of *service*. This included service to clients by providing them with more skilled representation. It also meant paying greater attention to those who were the nearest and dearest in my life. And, it included service to the greater communities in which I lived. Of the triad of silencing, self and service, the element of service was the easiest for me. At the same time, I realized my service would not be as worthwhile, satisfying or effective without sufficient time for silencing and self.

A few years ago I retired from the active practice of law, although I continue to stay in contact and work with lawyers all over the United States on various matters. From even a short distance, I see more and more the urgent, crucial need for balance in our lives as lawyers. Society depends on us for solving complex problems, settling disputes, and giving advice. This, I sincerely feel, can best be done when we are practicing law and living life in a harmonious manner.

Recently, my wife and I were instrumental in helping form a foundation at my firm for the purpose of matching the talents of lawyers, staff, alumni and their families with the needs of the communities where they live. In carrying out its mission, this foundation will help the people involved bring greater harmony into their very busy lives.

In closing, I earnestly believe that for our individual well being, for our relationship with those most important in our lives, for the welfare of our clients and for the greater good of society, we lawyers need to become more aware of and more proactive about the lack of equilibrium in our lives. Our family, colleagues, and friends can be of valuable assistance to us in this vital endeavor. We must never forget that we are much better able to teach what we live when we are on the Wheel of Life. I became conscious of the concept of the Wheel of Life and the need for balance relatively late in my practice. I am hopeful that future generations of lawyers will discover it much earlier.

There is always the danger that we may just do the work for the sake of the work.

Mother Theresa

Ode To Oliver

Linda Stephens*

O Lawyer as you toil and struggle,
It seems your life is full of trouble
From clients who demand too much
To never having time for lunch.

Your day begins, it never ends.
Seems such a waste to make amends
With adversaries who thrive on strife
Could be you've lost your appetite

For endless posturing and legal battle,
Before midday you're feeling rattled
Email, voice mail, cell phones, faxes
You want to scream and just plead laches!

---

* Linda Stephens is a partner with Teague, Campbell, Dennis & Gorham, L.L.P., in Raleigh, North Carolina, where she specializes in the defense of workers' compensation claims. To escape the pressure and demands of her job, and with the help of her husband, a Superior Court Judge, she rescues and nurses stray cats back to health. Oliver was found in a parking lot of a shopping center.

Then enter Oliver on padded paw.
Around this firm his purr is law.
Namesake of a famous scholar,
He ignores the billable dollar

To stretch instead and seek the sun.
He understands the need for fun.
The papers on the desk exist
To serve his goal to lounge in bliss.

His value here cannot be measured
The lessons learned forever treasured
Of balance, kindness, fun and frolic,
The need to stop and smell the garlic

Or whatever makes you curious!
Take a break from being furious!
Lawyering is so demanding
Find the means for gaining standing

To leave the press of work behind,
Escape the files and ease your mind
If only for a little while
The work will wait, so go in style.

Restore your strength, renew your spirit,
Star in a play, pen a lyric,
Hit some balls, read a book.
See a friend, learn to cook.

Upon return to office life,
You'll find it easier to handle strife.
Civility will come more quickly
Your adversary won't seem as filthy!

But, if you can't get out of town
Because the work has got you slammed,
There still are ways to decease stress
And thus ensure you'll do your best.

What works for me may not for you,
Though many trials have proved it true.
A purr, a rub, a flash of fur
All worries ease - it's Oliver

Reminding me to analyze
The issues and prioritize
My life between the work and play
Lest darkest night merge into day.

His green eyes beg the bigger question
And therein lies the larger lesson
To balance this with more of that,
I'm blessed to have my office cat!

We all, the most unbelieving of us, walk by faith. We do our work and live our lives not merely to vent and realize our inner force, but with a blind faith and trembling hope that somehow the world will be a little better for our striving.

Oliver Wendell Holmes

Serving "The Least Of These"

Jock M. Smith*

I had only been in practice for five years, when a case that would increase my faith in justice and direct my destiny as a lawyer visited my doorstep. In 1982, my law office was housed in a community action agency, called the Southeast Alabama Self Help Association (SEASHA). The Association's mission was to improve the economic and social lot of black people throughout twelve southeast Alabama counties. The director and founder of SEASHA came to me a few years earlier at the beginning of my law career and pledged his organization's support in helping me establish a law office. He told me that SEASHA was looking for a lawyer to help set up a practice for disenfranchised black people, who had been long term victims of the legal system. In return, I pledged to support SEASHA'S cause.

---

* Jock M. Smith is a Senior Partner in the law firm of Cochran, Cherry, Givens & Smith, with offices in Alabama, Atlanta, Los Angeles, and New York City. He concentrates in the area of plaintiffs' catastrophic injury cases. He is also the founder and CEO of "Scoring for Life," a motivational speaking company that directs youth to make better choices in life.

One day, the founder of SEASHA came to my office and asked me to become involved in a case in Tallapoosa County, Alabama. He informed me that a number of black families in that community were being taken advantage of, through immoral and illegal foreclosure actions, and that those families were in need of my immediate intervention. He also made it clear to me that SEASHA had very little money to pay for my services and that he was asking me to do it as a favor to him and to blacks. In my heart, I knew that I had to say "Yes."

After interviewing several of these families at my law office, I determined that they were in serious danger of losing their homes. The legal instrument at issue in the lawsuit was a "Bond For Title." In effect, this is a document stating that one receives a deed only after an entire indebtedness to the owner is paid off over an extended period of time. At that time, Bonds For Title were typical of the way many wealthy landowners would conduct business with poor folk. In some instances, landowners hoped that poor families would default somewhere along the line by making an untimely payment or two, so that immediate eviction from the premises would be legally in order. When I determined that all of these families had Bonds For Title rather than deeds to their respective homes, I became disheartened because

I realized that the chances of winning their cases were slim to none.

Initially, the cases against these families were filed in the District Court of Tallapoosa County. The District Court does not allow a trial by jury, but a trial before a sitting judge who is duly elected by the people of the county. Given the politics of Tallapoosa County and the political clout that the landowner carried, I knew that we would not prevail. Ultimately, we would have to appeal the case to the Circuit Court of Tallapoosa County, where we would request a trial by jury. The presiding judge confirmed this when he asked me to accompany him to lunch. On our journey back to the courthouse, he informed me of all the reasons why he intended to rule against me. I was quite unmoved by his recitation, as I had predicted it. In fact, the appropriate papers to appeal the matter to the Circuit Court of Tallapoosa County were already in my briefcase.

After the case was docketed with the Tallapoosa County Circuit Court via the appeal, I immediately entered defenses to the case under the legal theories of the Part Performance Doctrine and Estoppel. That is, these families made irregular payments on and off for twelve to fifteen year periods. Under Equity law in Alabama at that time, if these families had partly performed and were lead to believe by the acceptance of partial and/or late payments that the owner had accepted such a payment schedule, then he might be prohibited from foreclosing the property. With regard to Estoppel, Alabama law said that once the Part Performance Doctrine was proved by the defendants, the same possibly gave rise to the owner being stopped from evicting the individual with whom he was transacting business over the years. Though the defenses might seem cogent to the reader, keep in mind that Tallapoosa County was, and is, a predominately white jurisdiction, which did not have a history of justly protecting black folks like my clients. Thus, my outlook was pessimistic.

I remember the striking of the jury for our first case, just like it was yesterday. Two steeply entrenched local white lawyers represented the plaintiff, who was the wealthiest landowner in the county. I was representing a poor rural black family who had purchased their home approximately fifteen years earlier.

There were approximately thirty-six people in the jury pool, five of whom were black. Each side had twelve strikes. The landowner's counsel used up their first few strikes by excluding every potential black juror. As they made each strike, they would direct a grin in my direction as if to say, "Son, you have no chance. We are going to impanel a white jury who will seal your clients' doom before a word in the trial is spoken."

Keep in mind that this was proper jury selection at that time. Years later the United States Supreme Court would determine that striking jurors along racial lines without race neutral reasons was unconstitutional. However, on that hot summer day in 1982, my clients did not have that opportunity to experience such a privilege.

During the voir dire of the jury, I spent most of my time asking the potential jurors questions about whether or not they could be fair to my clients even if it meant deciding against the wealthiest white landowner in the county. I also inquired as to whether they could be fair to me in that I was a black lawyer, something that just did not exist in Tallapoosa County.

Though no jurors raised their hands informing me that they could not be fair, it was clear to me from the chilly atmosphere and the stone-faced responses I was receiving, that my clients and I would be the victims of a race based ruling. After the jury was chosen, I noticed that the only person remaining in the courtroom to view the trial was an elderly black woman with a cane, who seemed very attentive throughout the proceedings.

Shortly into the trial, the circuit judge who was presiding over the trial informed the counsel as to how he intended to instruct the jury. He told us that he was going to inform the jury that if the landowner won, then my clients would be immediately evicted from the property and the jury would only have to determine what the reasonable value of the rent was due to the landowner. The judge went on to say that if my clients prevailed, then they would own the homes outright and the eviction and/or foreclosure process would be avoided. Once the judge pronounced this, it was clear to me that part of my job was to have the value of the property in question assessed as low as possible in case we did not prevail.

The landowner called the most recognized and experienced real estate appraiser in Tallapoosa County as a key witness. The landowner's counsel got the witness to admit that he was well familiar with the homes in question. He testified that the homes were built in or around 1957, and that he had engaged in many real estate transactions involving these homes over the years, offering many appraisals. The witness also testified that the value of the property had gone up tremendously since 1957.

Accordingly, the witness certified that my clients owed a substantial sum in past due rentals, under the Bond For Title. The witness went on to proclaim that a reasonable rental in 1982 for the properties in question was substantially higher than the payments that my clients were even required to make under the Bond For Title agreement.

As bleak as the case appeared, I didn't give up. At the tail end of my cross-examination of this witness, I asked a series of questions that could have only come from the Master above. In summary, the questions and answers went as follows:

Question: "Sir, You have quite an impressive resume. Would it be safe to say that you are the Real Estate Guru of Tallapoosa County with regard to property appraisals?"

Answer: "Yes."

Question: "Would it be fair to say that you are the Alpha and the Omega, the essence and quintessence of real estate transactions and property values within the four corners of Tallapoosa County? Is that not so, Sir?"

Answer: "Yes."

Question: "Sir, you indicated that you are very familiar with the history of the property that is the subject matter of this lawsuit. Right?"

Answer: "Yes."

Question: "Sir, let me ask you this. What was the racial makeup of the community in 1957 when these homes were first built?"

Answer: (extended pause) "It was all white."

Question: "Sir, please tell me what is the racial makeup of this community today?"

Answer: (extended pause) "It's all black."

At this point the trial judge was sitting back in his seat almost choking on his cigar, smiling and wondering in his own mind whether I would have the courage to ask the last and final question that needed to be asked. After much reflection, I asked the final question in this way:

Question: "Sir, is it not a pragmatic principle of Alabama real estate that when us folks move in (pointing to myself) the value of property goes down?"

Answer: (after at least a minute pause) "That is true, Sir."

Final Statement: "Thank you, Sir. That ends my cross-examination at this time."

The judge called me to the bench with a big smile on his face saying, "I would have never believed that you had the guts to ask those questions." I informed the judge that it was my duty as a lawyer to represent my clients to the fullest extent of my abilities, even if it meant rehashing some of the racial issues of the past.

During my closing argument to the jury, I informed them that I was foolish enough to believe that the ink had not yet dried on the Declaration of Independence in Tallapoosa County, and that noble precepts of justice pervaded the county. I also said that I was foolish enough to believe that while my client and I were black, and that while the landowner was not only white, but the richest and most powerful landowner in the county, each of the jurors would still keep the promise they made under oath to be fair and impartial and decide this case based solely on the evidence. Looking straight at their detached faces, I asked this all white jury to pray before they rendered a decision in this case.

After about an hour and a half of deliberations, to everyone's surprise, the jury returned a verdict on behalf of my clients on every issue in the case. I believe the members of the jury searched their hearts and consciences and rendered a decision that they felt was just and fair in the instant case. They came down on the side of truth and resisted the temptation to come down on the side of prejudice.

As the members of the jury filed out very quietly, they were all looking at the ground, as if they themselves were in shock over the verdict they had just reached.

On my way out of the courtroom that evening, the elderly black woman with a cane in her hand, who had been sitting on the back row throughout the trial, approached me. She extended a handshake and said, "Son, I never thought I would see this day come in Tallapoosa County. God is going to bless you for what you have done here. If you continue to handle your cases this way, you will always be in His care and receive His abundant blessing."

"Ma'am," I said, "I'm not so sure that I thought I would ever see this day either. But I'm very proud to have been a part of it."

I was eternally rewarded and grateful for not only the outcome of the trial but for what it signified. Those twelve unknown souls of the Caucasian race, rendered a verdict of hope on that hot summer day. Their verdict represented the best of what America has to offer in its allegiance to the principles expressed in our Declaration of Independence, that "all men are created equal, that they are endowed by their Creator with certain unalienable Rights, that among these are Life, Liberty and the pursuit of Happiness."

This case affected families to whom Jesus referred as "the least of these." Now that more than seventeen years have gone by, there are many Rivers of Jordan still to be crossed on behalf of "the least of these," but I believe that one must first step into the water to truly understand the possibilities contained within.

Representing these families increased my faith and hope in the future, and relieved my despair. It showed me that a just cause *can* be won against all odds. It inspired me to try to help many other people since then and it will always remain part of my reason for practicing law.

The final test . . . . is battle in some form. . . . . It is one thing to utter a happy phrase from a protected cloister; another to think under fire -- to think for action upon which great interests depend.

Felix Frankfurter

Segregation : "What Is Past Is Prologue"

Collins J. Seitz[*]

As the legal profession reinvents itself in our rapidly changing society, today's lawyers are, like never before, in search of heroes and role models. Fortunately, I never had to search very far. My father acted as my compass for many years. By example, he helped me and my three siblings develop a heightened sensitivity to injustice at an early age. In addition, his behaviors taught us to appreciate the importance of honesty, civility, and compassion in the practice of law.

Well before the United States Supreme Court desegregated our schools, my father, while on the Delaware Court of Chancery, ordered the all white University of Delaware to admit applicants without regard to race and

---

[*] The Honorable Collins J. Seitz served on the Delaware Court of Chancery from 1946 until his appointment to the United States Court of Appeals for the Third Circuit in 1966. He served on the Third Circuit first as a Judge, then as a Chief Judge, and later as a Senior Judge until his death in 1998.

struck down segregation in two of Delaware's public schools. The latter decisions were among the five appeals consolidated with the Brown v. Board of Education case. The late Justice Thurgood Marshall labeled my father's decision in Belton v. Gebhart as the "the first real victory in our campaign to destroy segregation of American pupils in elementary and high schools."

Why did my father challenge traditional thinking about race relations? How does one develop such uncommon courage as a judge? My father partly answered these questions in the following speech, which he gave in 1990 at the University of Virginia, on the occasion of receiving the Thomas Jefferson Award in Law.

Collins J. Seitz, Jr.[†]

Any real appreciation of my desegregation decisions requires some understanding of the social attitude toward blacks and their legal status in Delaware at the time of those decisions. In 1950, Delaware's constitution required segregated public schools. Statutes and custom also helped to make segregation

[†] Collins J. Seitz, Jr. is a partner in the Wilmington, Delaware firm of Connolly Bove Lodge & Hutz, LLP.

a way of life for blacks living in Delaware. It was not dissimilar to the black-white relationships in the southern states: separate dining facilities, separate lodgings, separate social conditions, and, of course, separate schools at every level. Delaware was accurately described as a northern state with a southern exposure.

Thus, those educated in the white Delaware public schools had no real contact with blacks. Whites lived in a society largely satisfied with the status quo. My own background was not dissimilar. I was reared in a practically all-white suburban environment and had almost no personal contact with blacks.

Given my background, I have frequently been asked how I account for my subsequent sensitivity to the "white" man's problem in America. There is no ready explanation. I was not converted by a flash of light. It is true that I was the youngest of five boys and a child of the Great Depression. Both helped to qualify me for underdog status.

In addition, while attending the University of Virginia Law School, I witnessed two injustices that are still vivid in my mind over 50 years later. The first involved an intersection collision. A white driver went through a stop sign and struck a car driven by a black. The white policeman arrested the black.

The second recollection is of a bus ride from the University to downtown Charlottesville. It was early evening and the bus was filled with students who had taken all the seats and jammed the aisle from front to back. These, of course, were the days when blacks were required to go to the back of the bus. A black woman entered the bus and paid her fare. There was no way she could physically get to the back. Nevertheless, the white driver stopped the bus and castigated her mercilessly because she was forced to remain standing in the front.

How much these experiences contributed to my outlook on racial justice is a matter for psychologists to answer. My wife has a simple answer. She says my support for the underdog all stems from the fact that when I was growing up, I was a devoted fan of the perpetually losing Philadelphia Phillies baseball team. She insists that I thereby developed a strong empathy for the loser.

In 1940, when I joined the Delaware Bar, my first priority was to make a living. A few years later I was appointed Vice Chancellor in the Delaware Court of Chancery, a state-wide trial court with no jury that handled litigation involving Delaware corporations and general equity matters. I was all of thirty-one years of age at that time.

In 1950, several black plaintiffs filed suit in the Delaware Court of Chancery after being denied admission to the white University of Delaware. They alleged, inter alia, that it was vastly superior to Delaware State College for blacks and thus they were being deprived of an equal education. The Chancellor was a named defendant and the case came to me. At that time, I had been on the Court for about four years.

After a trial and review of the two institutions, I first determined in Parker v. University of Delaware, that because of Supreme Court precedent I could not say that the trustees' action was unconstitutional per se. I next compared the two institutions and concluded that the black college was grossly deficient in almost every meaningful element. To cap the comparison, the college was unaccredited. I determined, therefore, that the plaintiff class was being deprived of an equal education by the State.

The Attorney General's real defense in Parker was that, if the Court should find the black institution unequal to the University, it should adopt the traditional approach and order that the black college be made equal, but not permit admission of the black plaintiffs to the University of Delaware. The plaintiffs obviously contended to the contrary.

The relief requested by plaintiffs had not, so far as I knew, ever been granted at the undergraduate level in this country. I was nevertheless not persuaded that the black plaintiffs should be denied the fruits of their victory. To countenance delay was to deny them relief. I therefore enjoined the University and the trustees from considering race in processing applications for admission to the University. The Trustees did not appeal. Thus, in 1950, my undergraduate alma mater became an all-American University in fact and in law.

You may be surprised to be told that the adverse public reaction to my decision was minimal despite deep community bias. I believe the general population did not appreciate the significance of Parker because the University touched only a small number of white Delaware families.

However, in 1952, after I had become Chancellor, Belton v. Gebhart and Bulah v. Gebhart were filed in the Delaware Chancery Court seeking desegregation of an elementary and a secondary public school. I heard the cases together and was again confronted with the claim that legal segregation was per se unconstitutional and, if not, that the status of these schools nevertheless violated the separate but equal doctrine. After a protracted trial and review of the schools, which are described in detail in Richard Kugler's book entitled *Simple Justice*, I came to the moment of truth.

I first stated that I believed segregation was per se unconstitutional under the Equal Protection Clause. I then wrestled with the profound issue as to whether, despite my affirmative finding as to the psychological harm suffered by black children as a consequence of segregated schools, I was free to implement such a conclusion in view of Supreme Court precedent, which, of course, was binding on me. As my opinion states, I finally decided that I was not free to so rule in light of certain Supreme Court precedent. However, I went on to say that the declaration of invalidity should come from the United States Supreme Court. I never could see how the equal protection clause could be read any other way.

I next considered whether the segregated schools met the separate but equal test. The black plaintiffs in Belton lived in Claymont, Delaware, and sought to attend the white high school in their home area. In order to implement its segregation position, the Board of Education denied them admission to the white school. They were told, in effect, that they could go by bus to the black high school in Wilmington, some nine miles away.

I shall not recite the dreary facts that resulted in my determination that the black high school in Wilmington was grossly inferior to the Claymont school. The facts concerning the grade school involved in Bulah were even more disturbing because of the ages of the children involved. The comparison between the white and black schools left no room for doubt that separate was in all respects unequal, as my visit confirmed.

The incident that triggered the Bulah lawsuit teaches a lesson for all embryonic lawyers. I quote from my opinion:

> "School bus transportation is provided those attending No. 29 (White) who, except for color, are in the same situation as this infant plaintiff. Yet neither school bus transportation, nor its equivalent is provided this plaintiff even to attend No. 107 (Black). The State Board ruled that because of the State Constitutional provision for separate schools, a Negro child may not ride in a bus serving a white school."

Mrs. Bulah, the child's mother, testified that she originally had no intention of bringing suit to desegregate the white school. All she wanted was to have the "white" bus, which came by her house, pick up her seven-year-old child and deliver her to the black school. The Board of Education's refusal to grant Mrs. Bulah's modest request triggered a much more pervasive demand which resulted in the complete legal desegregation of the white school. The lesson to be learned from this inaction by the Board is simple, yet profound: Indifference or callousness to small problems often generates larger ones.

Having determined that the schools were not equal, I was confronted, once again, with a frontier issue in America as to whether the students should be admitted at once to the white elementary and secondary schools or be deprived of their established rights by giving the State time to correct the inequalities at some future date.

As in Parker, I felt that a declaration of rights without providing plaintiffs with a remedy would amount to a Pyrrhic victory for plaintiffs. I therefore ordered their immediate admission. This again apparently was the first time, after a finding of inequality, that blacks were admitted at once to the white schools at the elementary and secondary levels.

Because of its obvious implications, the decision was controversial and deeply resented. I vividly remember that a young teacher at the white elementary school came to see me after my decision. She had been teaching some type of dancing at the time of my visit to the school. She told me in the bitterest terms that she would not have conducted the class that day had she known I was going to take cognizance of it in my opinion. I felt sorry that a young teacher could entertain such bitterness.

My judgment on the application of the separate but equal doctrine and the admission of the plaintiffs to the "white schools" was affirmed by the Supreme Court of Delaware in 1952. My refusal of a stay was also affirmed and thus black students attended the so-called "white" elementary and secondary schools involved in the lawsuits. Thereafter, the United States Supreme Court granted a writ of certiorari in both cases and consolidated them for argument with Brown v. Board of Education and two other cases, all in federal courts.

In 1954 the Supreme Court handed down its memorable opinion in Brown v. Board of Education and the other cases, including the Delaware case. Simply put, it concluded that in the field of public education the doctrine of separate but equal has no place. Chief Justice Warren, speaking for a unanimous court, said the result was dictated as a matter of "simple justice" under the equal protection clause of the fourteenth amendment. Plessy v. Ferguson was legally interred.

It is a matter of great satisfaction to me that my judgments were the only ones affirmed by the Supreme Court that day. More to the point, the United States had come somewhat closer to keeping faith with its Declaration of Independence.

After I moved to the Court of Appeals in 1966, I sat on the famous Girard College case in Philadelphia, where the attack was on the "white" limitation on applicants for admission to the college created by Mr. Girard's will. Our court held that state action was involved and struck the white limitation. We were roundly accused of violating the sanctity of wills. The United States Supreme Court denied certiorari.

Has the promise of Brown v. Board of Education been realized? Certainly it has as to de jure segregation in public education and otherwise. But de facto segregation continued and that was no surprise.

It is far from clear from the viewpoint of either blacks or whites that judicial remedies have meaningfully accomplished their benign objectives. After all, those remedies really amount to social experiments whose merits cannot be measured with precision. Certainly, the jury is still out as to their long-range efficacy.

In addition, history teaches that, despite the most legitimate grievances, long-range solutions in race relations must ultimately be found in the hearts of the people, rather than in the courts. But, this is cold comfort to those experiencing injustice. Nevertheless, good will and the relentless striving toward racial justice in our society remain vitally important charges on all of us if our deeds are to match our words. In Robert Browning's eloquent words: "man's reach should exceed his grasp, or what's a heaven for?"

The Peacemaker

John O. Mudd*

My joy was boundless. I had learnt the true practice of law. I had learnt to find out the better side of human nature and to enter men's hearts. I realized that the true function of a lawyer was to unite parties driven asunder. The lesson was so indelibly burnt into me that a large part of my time during the twenty years of my practice as a lawyer was occupied in bringing about private compromises in hundreds of cases. I lost nothing thereby - not even money, certainly not my soul.

Mahatma Ghandi

Her heart was broken when she heard that her son, her daughter-in-law and her infant grandson had been killed by a truck. Each day since the automobile accident, she lived with the pain of her loss. She did

---

* John O. Mudd is a partner in the law firm of Garlington, Lohn & Robinson of Missoula, Montana. He was previously the Dean of the University of Montana School of Law. In addition to his law practice, he serves regularly as a mediator and arbitrator.

not understand much of the legal part of the tragedy, but she knew that the purpose of this meeting was to finish her claim against the trucking company involved in the accident so as to avoid going to court. Although she was middle-aged, this woman, whom I'll call Sarah, had the understanding of a young girl.

I was the mediator that day, attempting to resolve the wrongful death claims brought by the families of the three victims. Those of us involved in the mediation process knew that this mentally disabled mother would have difficulty understanding everything. However, Sarah had her lawyers and a close friend with her. They would help protect her legal rights.

As with any mediation involving tragedy, this one was emotional and sensitive. There were issues of comparative fault between the truck driver and the driver of the car. We also had to attempt the impossible: to place an economic value on the loss of a young family.

After a long day of going over these matters and negotiating settlement amounts, an agreement was reached. The trauma and pain of the accident would not have to be relived through a lengthy trial. No one would have to argue about the economics of this horrible loss of life. There was a profound sense of relief in the room.

Before leaving, I went to each person to express my thanks for the cooperation and effort that made the agreement possible. Because of her place at the large conference table, I came to Sarah last. I smiled and held out my hand. Sarah looked into my eyes, then threw her arms around me and hung on. We stood there for a few moments, linked to each other, as she said with her hug what she could not put into words.

In her simple, spontaneous expression of gratitude, this mother reinforced in me a critical point about my role as a lawyer. What she wanted most that day was to find healing over the deaths of her loved ones. Sarah did not want a court battle. She deserved the kind of justice that comes with peace, not the kind that is fought out in conflict and causes pain. The other parents expressed their relief and gratitude with adult words. Sarah's child-like hug, given without a sound, was the thanks and the lesson I cannot forget.

The world of law is filled with metaphors describing the lawyer's work in war-like terms. We do "battle" in court, "scorch" the earth with our discovery, "win" great victories, and endure painful "defeats." In this simple world of victors and vanquished, villains and victims, it is easy to become trapped in a contest of power where winning is everything.

As a young lawyer going off to trial, I found the warrior metaphor seductive. After juries disagreed with my clients' positions in a few cases, however, I began to have a deeper understanding of a hard truth. The purpose of a trial is not for jurors to judge who has the best lawyer. The jury's task, and one they take very seriously, is to find justice between competing claims. This is not war at all. It is a very human effort to resolve conflict fairly and peacefully.

Even though some of my clients wanted me to destroy the opposition, it began to dawn on me that my role as a lawyer was not to be a warrior. For all of its imperfections, the court system is intended to be an instrument of peace, not a process to make disputes worse by escalating them into war.

As I began to ponder these ideas, I also began to appreciate the words of a wise federal judge before whom I had the good fortune of practicing. He wrote that the longer he practiced law the more he came to understand that as a lawyer he was like "a can of oil." Using his skill he could help the daily life of his community run a little more smoothly. He could help take friction and heat out of human affairs. To play a part in creating a more tranquil and peaceful community was for him a noble calling.

This perspective requires that the lawyer consider not just legal issues, but the human issues in any conflict as well. For example, in many situations the parties must continue to work together after a particular dispute is resolved. Patching over the conflict with a legal solution may resolve some issues, but the very process of reaching a legal solution that is acrimonious and protracted may aggravate the underlying conditions that led to the dispute in the first place. If the lawyer appreciates only the legal issues in a conflict, the root cause will return later like a bad dream.

While writing this essay I received two unexpected letters. One woman wrote to thank me for helping settle her employment case. She wanted me to know that settling her lawsuit had made unexpectedly dramatic differences in her life. A burden had been lifted from her, and without that extra weight she had been able to get her life back together.

With the second letter was enclosed a picture of a mother and her grown children, all smiling as they celebrated her birthday. The happy scene would have been unthinkable only a few weeks earlier when they were headed to court as adversaries. Their dispute had been settled because their attorneys did not engage in battle. They used their professional skills to find a way for a mother to live her final years in peace with her children and grandchildren.

Obviously, not every dispute can be resolved as these were. Some parties are unable to reach agreement by themselves, so a judge or jury must decide the matter for them. But even in preparing and presenting a case to the court, the lawyer with the perspective of a peacemaker will walk the path of civility.

Our calling as peacemakers is at the heart of our profession. Because the law deals with human relationships, the lawyer must serve those relationships. When relationships become strained or are broken, lawyers can help bring reconciliation and restore harmony. This essential work is not a byproduct of war. It comes from seeking peace.

Dear Grandson, With Regard To Becoming A Lawyer.....

Ronald L. Snow*

It is a spectacularly sunny summer afternoon in New Hampshire, complete with a slight breeze and low humidity. I sit in an overflowing church at a memorial service for the late Robert H. Reno, my dear friend and one of two founders of our law firm some fifty-two years ago. You, my first grandson, were just born far away in Montana. Whereas daily pressures keep us from taking a few moments for thoughtful contemplation, momentous events such as deaths and births force us to do so. And so it is not surprising that I am experiencing a mixture of bittersweet memories about the past and fond hopes for your future. I am filled with thoughts and feelings that I would like to share with you.

---

* Ronald L. Snow is the senior trial lawyer at the firm of Orr & Reno, P.A., Concord, New Hampshire. Educated at Dartmouth College, BA 1958, and Yale University Law School, JD 1961, he is a founding member of the Daniel Webster Chapter of the American Inns of Court, the New Hampshire Chapter of the American Board of Trial Advocates, and a Fellow of the American College of Trial Lawyers.

As the memorial speakers recount Bob Reno's professional achievements, I wonder what I might say to you, Jack, if you were to ask at some point whether you should consider law for yourself. I realize that I have been associated with Bob for thirty-seven of his fifty-two years at the bar. I think to myself, "What is it that stands out about his life and career that is most important?" As I ponder this question, for some reason, I first consider what is not all that important. For example, the pure technical, legal skill which earned Bob a lifetime achievement award from the New Hampshire Bar Association doesn't seem as significant in my thoughts as the style in which he practiced his profession for all those years.

What I remember most is Bob's civility and his passion. He was civil to all around him, friend and foe alike. He was consistently passionate about his clients' causes and the principles of law and order. Robert Reno's name is listed as representing clients in several New Hampshire Supreme Court cases. The one that stands out, however, involved three trips to the Supreme Court for one client until he was satisfied the client had received a fair and just result.

Bob was an avid, low-handicap golfer; but what his closest friends remember about their outings was the charm and true collegiality that he brought to each round. He was as competitive on the golf course as anyone you could imagine, but at the end of the day, the score card was unimportant. In a word, he was fun to be around.

There is no doubt that Bob came to New Hampshire in 1946 with excellent credentials: Dartmouth College, Yale Law School, service in the military as a Marine aviator, and even a tour with the FBI. What gave him a chance at true success and happiness, however, was the opportunity to practice law and thereby influence the lives of countless people. His sense of fairness and ethics complemented his skill and intelligence. I remember Bob refusing a new set of golf clubs from a grateful client on one occasion on the grounds that he couldn't accept a gift unless he could share it with his partners.

Yes, Bob was successful because he was a good, hard working man who respected the law. In the final analysis, he was successful because his causes, his friends, his colleagues, and his family were more important than his balance sheet.

One of the things you may hear about my profession is that many people who practice law don't really like it. You also may hear that lawyers don't care about their clients and basically want only to get rich and have nice homes and large boats.

Jack, one of the reasons some people are unhappy practicing law is that they come into the profession for the wrong reasons. Yet, I've been in this business for a long time and have enjoyed it immensely. I still look forward to most days, but I am not and will never be a multi-millionaire.

As far as the public image of lawyers is concerned, some of it is deserved. But the overwhelming majority of attorneys whom I know personally are honest and helpful to others. Many times, they even help people for free.

When I joined my firm, the more experienced partners not only taught me the law, but they also taught me about respect for the concept of right and wrong. They explained to me that taking a shortcut for a short-term gain is not the way to build a lasting reputation. They convinced me that my reputation is the most important possession I own. It is like an ancient Chinese vase, very valuable but very fragile; it is never the same even with the tiniest crack.

Maybe I can best answer the question about whether law is a profession worth considering by telling you what has given me the most personal pleasure in this work: solving people's problems. The single most exciting case of my young career was representing, for no fee, a young man accused of murder in the first degree. Fortunately for me and the client, I was the junior member of a three-person team representing the defendant.

The deceased and our client had a "gunfight" at 5:00 p.m. on a Saturday evening at a used car lot called "The OK Corral," over the affections of the client's wife. The other man had run off with our client's bride while he was in North Carolina training with the First Airborne Division.

The attorney general of the state was the lead prosecutor and demanded the death penalty, which in those days resulted in hanging. Our client had clearly killed the other man and there was no hope for a complete acquittal. Our strategy was to prove that our client felt justifiable rage over the decedent's skullduggery. Proving that would eliminate the legal element of malice; we wanted to show the jury that although this man had made a horrible mistake, he was not evil at heart.

When the jury returned to the courtroom, I stood next to the defendant and began to feel physically ill. A young man's life was in the balance. I remember the tightness in my throat; I wasn't breathing and the clock sounded like a gong each time it ticked. As to the charges of murder in the first or second degree, the foreman said "Not guilty." Manslaughter was our goal. Manslaughter was the result!

John served about three years in prison. While there, we got him a job as the first work release prisoner in New Hampshire history. The kind warden released John to my custody every other weekend, to perform odd jobs. John baby-sat your dad, took him swimming, and became part of our family. After being released from prison, he went to college, remarried, had a family, and is now a successful accountant.

A second memorable case of mine involved a lady named Judy who had a stroke at age twenty seven and was paralyzed on one side of her body as a result. She had suffered severe brain damage and her life was completely changed. Judy's physician had prescribed a high-dose birth control pill for her for a number of years, and, after her stroke, believed that there had to be a connection between the medication and her stroke. He came to this conclusion after realizing that there had been an unusually large number of problems in patients who used these products.

The problem with taking on one of these cases against a national pharmaceutical company was twofold: First, a little research made it clear that although there had been a few plaintiffs' verdicts in these cases, there had not been, up to that time, any successful verdict that had survived the appellate process. Secondly, for a small firm, the financial risk of what was clearly anticipated to be a major piece of litigation was substantial.

The case took over five years to pursue through trial and two appeals, but resulted in the first million-dollar verdict in this jurisdiction. The reason I list this case as one of my favorites, however, has to do with much more than the verdict or amount of money awarded. Before the case ended, Judy was without hope and depressed, and we all feared that she might not be able to cope with the stresses of daily living. After the case ended, we helped her invest her funds properly and she has lived happily on them ever since. She has become a leader in support groups for stroke victims in this state and now solves problems for others. My role in this case continues to give me pleasure every time I see her.

In summary, law still is a noble profession, worthy of the best efforts of the best people. It's not meant for everyone, but if you choose it and treat it with respect, it will be rewarding. The main thing you will need to consider in entering the profession of law is whether your primary goal is to serve others. Come to think of it, that is the main thing you will need to consider no matter what career you choose. I have learned that acts of kindness are the ultimate measures of one's success, and in turn, one's happiness. My dear grandson, I wish you much happiness.

There is a vague popular belief that lawyers are necessarily dishonest. I say vague, because when we consider to what extent confidence and honors are reposed in and conferred upon lawyers by the people, it appears improbable that their impression of dishonesty is very distinct and vivid. Yet the impression is common, almost universal. Let no young man choosing the law for a calling for a moment yield to the popular belief -- resolve to be honest at all events; and if in your judgment you cannot be an honest lawyer, resolve to be honest without being a lawyer. Choose some other occupation, rather than one in the choosing of which you do, in advance, consent to be a knave.

Abraham Lincoln

Never Stop Reaching And Growing

Paul G. Ulrich*

Thirty-nine years ago, while sitting at a secluded study carrel in the old Stanford Law School library, I often wondered why I ever decided to go into law, and how my career would turn out. The novelty of the Socratic method classes had quickly worn off during that first semester, and my fear was on the rise. I was becoming increasingly apprehensive about learning all of the material being presented day by day, and whether all of the time I was spending on studying would ever pay off.

Given the pressures we were under, a number of first-year students with excellent undergraduate records had already dropped out. Everyone else was wondering who would be next. Based on coffee room conversations, I was convinced that many of my classmates knew far more than I did. I was

---

* Paul G. Ulrich is the founding shareholder of Ulrich & Anger, P.C., in Phoenix, Arizona. His practice involves state and federal civil appeals and related litigation. He is a general co-editor and contributor for the "Arizona Appellate Handbook," and co-author of "Federal Appellate Practice: Ninth Circuit." He is also the author of numerous articles and has spoken at many programs concerning appellate practice and law practice management.

unsure about whether I would be able to handle six more months of this type of stress without knowing what my grades would be.

I now feel nostalgic about that time. As I write this chapter, I have a fantasy of being able to put my hand on the shoulder of that 23-year-old first-year law student of my past, and talking with him like a loving father does with his son. The advice I would offer goes something like this:

One of the lessons you will learn is illustrated in Stephen Sondheim's musical, "Into the Woods." Its first act simultaneously dramatizes five well known fairy tales, but with a twist. The lives of each set of characters begin to intertwine, and their stories become both more convoluted and humorous, as they each go "into the woods" to complete their appointed tasks. Nonetheless, each story is more or less completed in its original form by the end of Act One, and everyone seems to be ready to "live happily ever after."

Wrong. Act Two is filled with crises. Characters are killed and blinded, and existing relationships are destroyed. However, new relationships are formed, and the musical achieves a somewhat happy ending. As one of the characters states, its moral is that despite all the losses, happiness is achieved as the survivors learn to love and take care of each other.

Like those characters, we all have pre-programmed scripts for Act One of our lives: to succeed in college and law school, to get married and to start our careers. But playing out those scripts doesn't mean we'll "live happily ever after." Inevitably, there will be multiple crises to confront that we cannot anticipate. It's then up to us to make the necessary adjustments. No one else can do it for us. It's even better to decide on our respective "second acts" before, not after, our first ones end. Throughout our lives, though, we must keep growing, learning, developing, and renewing ourselves. You are only at the beginning of your education in life, not at its end.

Another lesson you will learn is exemplified in the scene from Lewis Carroll's "Alice in Wonderland," in which the Cheshire Cat tells Alice that if she doesn't know where she is going, it doesn't make any difference which road she takes. Baseball player Yogi Berra put the same idea even more plainly: "If you don't know where you're going, you're going to end up somewhere else." Others have expressed similar conclusions. For example, Henry David Thoreau wrote, "if one advances confidently in the direction of his dreams, and endeavors to live the life which he has imagined, he will meet with success unexpected in common hours." My grandfather kept this quotation from Bruce Barton's writings on his office wall: "I do not like the phrase 'never cross a bridge till you come to it.' The world is owned by men who cross bridges in their imaginations, miles and miles in advance of the procession."

How do you decide what accomplishments to pursue? Let me answer that question with a story. When he was a young college professor, a now well-known management consultant and author, David Maister, asked a senior faculty member what he had to do to receive tenure. He was told to focus on being the best at what he wanted to do. Maister then asked what he should focus on. The senior professor responded: "It's up to you. Do whatever you enjoy. Don't choose something you don't enjoy just because you think it's what we want." Maister later learned to appreciate the wisdom of this advice. If you don't enjoy what you do, how can you ever call it *success*?

Another lesson to learn early in your career is that life can and should be a continuous growth experience involving both setting and achieving goals, and enjoying life along the way as well. Psychologist Abraham Maslow's writings often discussed "self-actualizing" persons. These are people able to achieve their full potentials. One of the distinguishing qualities of self-actualizers is that they consider means and ends to be equally important. That is, they tend to focus on enjoying the journey as well as the destination.

You also will need to learn the art of principle-based goal setting and time management. As described by another well-known author and consultant, Stephen Covey, the most important time management instrument is not a clock, but an inner compass. The idea is that the quality of our lives is shaped significantly by whether we recognize what is most important to us, and act in accordance with our values. In addition, our goals need to be aligned with an honest assessment of our own personal skills, aptitudes, and interests.

One of the most important adjustments you will need to make is to develop a way of dealing with constant change. In case you haven't already noticed, the pace of change in your time has been accelerating, particularly because of the development of electronic tools that speed up and expand human communication.

The legal services in which you will be involved by the end of this century will bear little resemblance to the 1961 Stanford Law School course catalog. Most of what you will be doing isn't listed there at all. New concepts, cases, and statutes also will cause the specific information presented in your current classes to become obsolete. Succeeding in a rapidly changing legal environment will require you to develop core competencies that are both broader and deeper than subject matter knowledge in specific fields. Competencies such as written and oral advocacy, negotiating, litigation and appellate strategy, and project organization and management, can be applied to a wide variety of specific subject matter situations as required. Another critical core competency you will need is the ability to efficiently find and make use of constantly changing information.

It will be easy for you to continue to provide professional services as you've always done. However, at some point your knowledge and skill may become outdated, or someone else may appear on the scene who can provide your service faster, better and cheaper. Thus, you must constantly improve your services. Doing so in turn will require you to develop specialized knowledge about clients' industries, and to constantly build both your technical and counseling skills.

Form the habit of asking your clients for feedback on how you've performed. Also, periodically ask yourself some questions: "In what way am I personally more valuable in the marketplace than last year? What specific new skills do I plan to acquire or enhance in the next year? What's my personal strategic plan for the next three years? What, precisely, is it that I want to be famous for?"

Finally, Paul, you will need to learn that you can't do it all by yourself. You will need to "leverage" your own energy and skills by working with others to achieve mutual goals. This will require you to develop leadership skills. Leadership is more than simply a set of desirable personal attributes. To be effective, leaders must focus on achieving specific and objective results. Your strategy also has to include balancing the needs of your employees, clients, partners or shareholders, and your organization as a whole, in relation to your larger community.

Learn to delegate. Doing so will multiply your effectiveness many times in that it will give you more time to provide leadership. You must also learn to adjust your leadership style to your subordinates' needs. Initially, specific direction and goal-setting may be required for subordinates. However, over time, your goal should be to progressively reduce your intensity of supervision and help others become increasingly self-directed and autonomous. As a result, they will receive much greater personal job satisfaction and integrate their personal and organizational goals.

I know that right now it seems that your goal is to become independent, self-sufficient and in control. For now, there's nothing wrong with that. Within a few years, however, you will discover that there is yet a higher goal than independence. Steven Covey calls it "interdependence." To become truly successful you will need to fully appreciate the fact that none of us are truly independent. If we were, we'd be living by ourselves in caves, eating only animals we killed or plants we gathered personally. Our quality of life, and fulfillment of our fundamental needs and capacities, are interdependent with others. Choosing to work cooperatively with others is to everyone's greatest mutual advantage.

Having a shared vision with others can create a passion of synergistic empowerment, combining the energy and talents of all involved. It bonds people together, providing a sense of unity and purpose that in turn provides great strength in times of challenge. I urge you to develop such relationships whenever possible.

These are just some of the things you will need to learn about the ways to succeed at law. Of course, there are many other aspects of your life that you will need to attend to in order to truly succeed, such as balancing your professional life with a personal one, and never doing anything to damage your reputation for integrity. The main thought that I want to leave you with is that while it is true that no one can fully predict the future, the most effective way of coming close to it is to work consciously to create your desired future, both for yourself and those around you.

Leading The Way

Daniel E. Wathen*

"I am of the opinion that my life belongs to the whole community and as long as I live it is my privilege to do for it whatever I can."
George Bernard Shaw

As a young boy growing up in northern Maine in the 1950's, I never gave much thought to leadership. There were twelve hundred people in my town and we all thought we were in charge, or at least not following anyone. Always ready to challenge authority, I was an unmotivated and rebellious youth, complete with motorcycle, leather jacket, dungarees, and engineer's boots. After an uneven academic performance, having flunked out of college twice, I achieved some prominence in law school, and eventually developed a reputation as a successful lawyer.

---

* Daniel E. Wathen is the Chief Justice of the Maine Supreme Judicial Court and has been on the bench in Maine for twenty-two years. Recently, he has served as Chair of the Board of the National Judicial College, and he has been actively engaged in an effort to improve the manner in which courts serve families and children.

The practice of law taught me little about leading other people. A trial lawyer is a lone gladiator. Being a judge, which came next in my life, is also a solo endeavor. By design, judges view decision making as their individual responsibility, and go to great lengths to avoid being influenced by public reaction. Coming from this background, it is perhaps understandable that I never gave much thought to leadership.

Suddenly, at the age of fifty-two, after twelve years in private practice, four years on the trial bench, and eleven years on the Supreme Court, I was given the opportunity to lead the third branch of Maine's government. That brought the subject of leadership into sharp focus. Now I was faced with the following question: How do you influence the behavior of fifty appointed judges and four hundred staff members located at fifty widely scattered court locations?

I began my task with the mistaken notion that a leader is someone who has all the answers. As I visited all fifty courts in Maine, the first thing I learned was that I needed to become a better listener and to respond with smart questions rather than smart answers. Too often we fail not because our answer is wrong, but rather because we do not ask the right question. Silence is not something to fear.

Having visited the courts and convinced myself that no single person could influence a court system, I stopped in to see a friend of mine. Buzzy Fitzgerald, a fellow trial lawyer, who changed careers in mid–life to become the CEO of Maine's largest employer and defense contractor. His advice was simple: “You have to learn to tolerate a very high level of confusion.”

At first, I misunderstood and thought he was suggesting that the world is confused. Then I learned that his advice was more profound. Because human affairs are complex and each of us is unique, there is seldom a unanimous view on any subject. Meaning and truth are multifaceted and exist on several levels. My job is to organize it and honor it all. When I am at my best, I am like a modem; a great deal of information passes through me and it is my job to assemble it and direct it to the proper destination.

Soon after I became Chief Justice, we began a system-wide effort to draft a mission statement. In this process, someone made the simple point that you lead by your values. I wondered whether that meant that the court system would grow to reflect my values?

If I needed any confirmation of the connection between personal and organizational values, I only had to consider Maine's leading retailer L.L. Bean. Leon Gorman, a grandson of the founder and president of this family–owned retailing giant, is a friend and fishing companion. The L.L. Bean organization walks, talks, smells, and feels like Leon Gorman, a quiet and gentle man of quality. Through his example, I came to realize that if I wanted a court system that operated on the basis of honesty, openness, candor, and respect, then I needed to personally honor those values and model them on a daily basis. In the beginning, this was both a sobering and a frightening thought.

I also learned that I needed to keep my ideas simple. Complex theories and detailed strategies are entertaining, but only a few simple ideas have the capacity to transform our world and truly make a difference. My administrative function was to translate complex legal needs into simple ideas that could be easily conveyed to everyone in Maine.

With time, I learned that to be a leader I had to first become a servant. In addition, I had to learn to view the world through the eyes of those who work in the court system and those who are affected by it. For this reason, I sit in the trial courts periodically and someday soon I will work in the offices of the clerks. I also volunteer in a local soup kitchen, where at one time my supervisor was a chef on work release from the county jail. There is no better way to maintain a servant's perspective than to serve good food to hungry people.

Because I am completely dependent on four hundred and fifty other people to do my job, it is important that I give them my trust and provide appropriate praise and recognition for their efforts. It is seductively easy and ultimately meaningless to thank everyone for everything. It takes a lot of time and effort to provide praise that is genuine and sincere, but nothing else works.

In learning to lead, I have also learned valuable lessons about myself. Even though I am more than normally sensitive to criticism, I try to accept responsibility for all failures, while sharing all successes and always accompanying them with praise and recognition. Winston Churchill is supposed to have said that success is often nothing more than moving from one failure to another with undiminished enthusiasm.

I have also found that there are limits to my levels of energy, and that I need to withdraw periodically to break the rhythms. I don't care whether it is called the Sabbath or a day off, but I can only work two weeks in a row without a complete day off. Without it, I lose my effectiveness and become negative and irritable.

Finally, I have learned that one of the secrets of motivating others is to be passionate yourself. I was speaking at a forum designed to improve the delivery of civil legal services to Maine's poor. I quoted Rev.

Martin Luther King, Jr. in proposing that we need to create two visions: one depicting the way things are and another the way things should be. Then, we need to dare to tell the truth about the difference. I finished by adding, "and if we can't do that............." At this point I choked up a little. To be more accurate, the Chief Justice cried in front of a few hundred people.

I knew that some people were visibly moved, but I felt uneasy about showing my emotions. The next day, one of my colleagues complimented me on my speech and the passion I displayed. Embarrassed, I responded jokingly, "Yes, I was so intent on moving them that I made a mistake and moved myself." Little did I know it, but that was exactly the right thing to do.

Well, this summarizes the first seven years of my journey as Chief Justice. The things I have learned so far are applicable to all lawyers in leadership positions. Indeed these lessons are applicable to all leaders.

My bottom line is simple: The successful leaders of tomorrow will lead by the values they exemplify. They will not be authoritarian figures issuing commands and directives, supported by hierarchy. Instead, they will understand the necessity of including people and of valuing their continuing ability to learn, change, and grow. Effective leaders will seek to be accessible servants who engage others in dialogue and motivate them to commit to a shared vision.

It is my understanding that there is a meaningful connection between the words "leadership" and "education." That is, the literal meaning of the word "educate" is to lead out. I think that real leaders always seek the truth and attempt to communicate that truth to others in elegantly simple terms. I close with a quote that I think makes this point well:

> *Great ideas, it has been said, come into the world as quiet as doves. Perhaps, then, if we listen attentively, we shall hear, amid the uproar of empires and nations, a faint flutter of wings, the gentle stirring of life and hope.*
>
> *Albert Camus*

I find the great thing in this world is not so much where we stand, as in what direction we are moving. To reach the port of heaven, we must sail sometimes with the wind and sometimes against - but we must sail, and not drift, nor lie at anchor.

Oliver Wendell Holmes

Is The Future What It Used To Be?

C. Thomas Wyche*

Our South Carolina law firm, Wyche, Burgess, Freeman & Parham, was established in 1854 and has been described as an "old-fashioned family practice," even though today we have no lawyers who are related to each other. Nowadays, you can become "old-fashioned" overnight. Given all the mergers and subsequent downsizing, many law firms are here one day and gone the next. Deliberation and patience seem like lost virtues in an age dominated by e-mail and fax. Businesses and personal relationships on every level are being affected by change that is occurring at a frenetic pace.

The most significant change affecting law firms has been an increasing malaise, particularly among young lawyers. Idealism, dreams, careers, even families, are

---

*C. Thomas Wyche (Tommy) has practiced corporate, securities, tax, merger and acquisition law for more than 50 years in Greenville, South Carolina. He received his undergraduate degree in engineering from Yale University, his law degree from the University of Virginia, and was admitted to the South Carolina bar in 1948 at age 22. He holds honorary doctorate degrees from Clemson University, Furman University, and Wofford College.

becoming lost or abandoned as economic pressures, particularly billable hours, take their toll. Magazine headlines scream that "law is hell" and that the practice of law is like being in a "state of war."

Lawyers don't seem to be the only ones suffering. According to Fortune magazine, in an article published in February of 1999, "a new trend is emerging: In corporate America 40 is starting to look and feel old." The author of the article goes on to give an example of two major accounting firms that merged and subsequently fired 99 partners over the age of 40 and hired 122 younger partners.

Our firm is nearly 150 years old but our longevity does not immunize us from the changes occurring in society and the legal profession. In recent years, two lawyers have left our firm for other vocations, and two have gone with another law firm. Getting together, even for a coffee break, is becoming increasingly less routine. Like other folks, we wonder about our future. Is it what it used to be?

The purpose of this essay is to share our view that the ability of law firms to maintain a professional, as distinguished from purely economic, approach to the practice of law will depend on the quality of the relationships among their lawyers and between the lawyers and the firm's clients. We believe that the strong relationships that exist within our small firm will ensure our survival and help us flourish in changing times.

We make no claim that our past and present situation is superior to that of any other firm. However, over the course of our firm's existence, we have developed a value system that nurtures our relationships. We cultivate relationships that promote individual self-worth, particularly in young lawyers. Our communication with each other is clear, frank, and without guile. We try to relate to our clients and to the world in an open and trusting way. It is our opinion and hope that these values will guide us toward a successful future.

In describing our experiences, we do not intend to convert any firm to our way of practicing law. Moreover, we make no claim that we are a congenial Utopia existing apart from the pressures of the world. Our objective is to pose the question, "Is the future practice of law what it used to be?" By discussing this question, perhaps we can stimulate other lawyers to consider their own practices. In addition, we hope to encourage lawyers to reflect on the cause of the widespread general dissatisfaction with the practice of law and on whether any effort should be made within the Bar to deal with this problem.

Self-Worth

Healthy relationships begin with lawyers who have a high degree of self-worth. This view has shaped our recruiting and compensation process for decades. Historically, we have used a short open letter to attract young lawyers to consider our firm. In the letter, we explain that young lawyers at our firm will experience a wide range of activities and responsibilities beginning in their first year of practice. We say that although we do work hard, we are by no means addicted to work, and that we genuinely enjoy working with each other. More importantly, we try to make certain that prospective members of our firm understand that success is not measured on the basis of billable hours. Furthermore, we explain that the number of hours billed by our lawyers are not even known to its members and that compensation is not based on the amount of legal work brought to the firm.

We hire only those lawyers whom we expect will become members (partners) of the firm. We have a distaste for the practice of hiring associates with the idea of parting ways in five to seven years, having used their talents for our financial gain. The young lawyers who decide to join our firm are immediately treated as future members, not as profit centers. They experience a wide range of activities and responsibilities in their first year of practice and are accorded the respect and trust that are the foundation of the cordial relationships we have with each other. Except for discussions of internal finances, there is no differentiation between associates and members.

Associates participate at our weekly breakfast meetings and take their turn with all other lawyers in presiding over them. They interview prospective law clerks and associates. During the discussions on the pros and cons of these prospects, their views are voiced and respected equally with those of the members. It is understood that everyone is on a first name basis.

A "boss-employee" relationship is never cultivated because we operate on the basis that we are all professionals. These kinds of relationships are important in developing a feeling of camaraderie among our lawyers, seniors and juniors alike.

So far we have managed to avoid the pernicious sort of white-collar exploitation that occurs when hiring is based on the pyramid model. Our associates are hired to meet the needs of a growing client base and workload. They have never been hired to increase the income of the members. Finger pointing for inadequate production and complaints of uneven workload are not a part of our tradition. None of us aspires to great wealth through inflated incomes, particularly if they are derived from excessive amounts of billable hours from associates.

We do not suggest that at times our lawyers, young and old, do not burn the midnight oil and spend some weekends at work. We pride ourselves on spending whatever time is necessary to do the task the client needs done. We work hard at times, but only to meet the clients' needs, not to create billable hours.

Increasingly, we believe that young lawyers throughout the country are being valued not so much for their comprehension and love of the law, as for their endurance and ability to produce billable hours. Some young lawyers we have interviewed have told us that their overriding goal is to endure the pressures of large firm life only for a few years, until they repay their school loans and other debts. Then, it is their intention to leave the practice of law. One young applicant described it as a "zero sum game where you kill yourself in law school for three years; burn yourself out at a large firm for three years; then quit the job and give up the practice of law, disillusioned with the profession. In six years, you are back to ground zero."

Several research studies on the state of the legal profession in recent years have found a distressing level of disillusionment with the practice of law. For example, in a survey reported by the North Carolina Bar Association in 1991, twenty-six percent of its members would not choose the practice of law again, if given the choice, and only fifty-four percent wished to remain in law practice for the remainder of their careers.

In a 1998 study done by the National Association for Legal Placement, it was found that forty-three percent of associates leave their firms within three years of being hired. A report of the Boston Bar Association Task Force on Professional Challenges and Family Needs, published in 1999, concluded that "many law students, law firm associates and partners currently believe that being a successful partner or associate in private practice is incompatible with daily involvement in family life." This state of the practice of law should be of concern to all lawyers; it certainly does concern us.

In some firms, senior lawyers may be faring no better than young lawyers. As professionals, we will be greatly saddened if law firms, both large and small, cease to appreciate the client base and the firm's reputation created by the lifelong service of its senior partners. Will we be guided only by the question, "What have you done for me lately?" Hopefully, our firm will hold to its view that even when a senior partner's contribution to the firm's profit becomes negligible and his income is commensurately diminished, he will not be summarily retired to save the expense of office space.

Although it is certainly not the trend today, we feel that practicing lawyers must do a better job in valuing each other. We must be realistic however, because changing economic paradigms is a difficult task. One promising hope could lie with law schools. Before entering the profession, law students should learn the significance of joining firms with pyramid structures, and the negative consequences that occur when the goal of partners is to profit from the earnings of associates. Students should be informed of the consequences of the pyramid structure, and the correlation between compensation and billable hours, regardless of the size of the firm. Only then, can they make an informed choice about employment.

Merely reducing the typical starting salary and billable hour requirement by twenty-five percent could make a big difference in job satisfaction and give lawyers adequate time for family and community projects. Maybe such ideas are too idealistic to survive in today's world, but we must remember that the future of our profession depends on the quality of the lawyers we develop.

Communication

There are two bedrock tenets in our firm's value system. First, we keep hours billed and fees collected known only to the billing lawyer. Second, we do not keep any records of fees vis-à-vis compensation, and no member monitors the hours billed or fees generated by our lawyers. In our view, to compare individual billings would fundamentally and irrevocably alter the firm for the worse. As a recent experiment, one senior partner is being furnished with the number of hours billed by each lawyer, but that lawyer keeps this information entirely confidential. The idea is that this lawyer can help the Compensation Committee avoid a mistake in its deliberations, yet do so without divulging the confidential data.

Traditionally, all firm billings have gone into a general income fund that has been allocated among the members and associates of the firm. The considerations in setting the percentage for each member of the firm have been based largely on seniority, and to a lesser degree, on several subjective factors, including the needs of younger members and other specific information gained by the compensation committee during the interviewing process.

The percentage for each member is a prospective division of fees, subject to the considerable uncertainties of income for the upcoming year. The agreed-on percentage remains in place, however, regardless of whether the projected fees are realized or not.

If there was ever any disagreement in regard to compensation, it occurred when a partner demurred and insisted that his percentage of partner income should be less. We know from C. Granville Wyche, who joined the firm in 1923 and led the firm until his death in 1986, that this philosophy of consensus and fair play permeated the firm during his sixty-three-year tenure. It is still followed today.

Although it has never been a deliberate part of the plan, it certainly has been the case that in some years the senior members of the firm have "worked for" the younger members and sometimes even for the associates, rather than the other way around. One year, when we admitted a couple of new members, we reminded them that membership, by definition, was a sharing of profits *and* losses and it might be the case that at times they would make less than an associate. This was said largely in jest, but as it turned out, that was just what happened. That year, we didn't make as much as we had projected and individual income for all members of the firm, including the newly admitted members, was less than the previous year.

Now that the firm has grown to twenty-seven lawyers, the philosophy of compensation has not changed, but the method of determining individual salaries is a more protracted process. There is a Compensation Committee that starts the process by conducting private interviews with each member and then making tentative salary recommendations for all the members and associates.

In preparing its recommendations, the Committee has no knowledge of the billable hours or the income generated by the individual member, except as a member might choose to disclose such information in the interview process. We continue to avoid compensation based principally on total revenue generated or hours billed by any lawyer. Nevertheless, based on individual interviews, discussions within the Committee, and guidance from a senior attorney with privileged information, hours billed and generated revenue has become one of numerous factors considered in the process.

After the tentative proposed salary structure is distributed, the Committee has a follow-up discussion with each member to evaluate his or her feelings about the tentative salary distributions within the firm. The Committee makes adjustments and then submits its final recommendations to the entire membership at a meeting held for that purpose.

At this meeting, the compensation of members, associates, and staff are agreed upon. All members are free to and expected to voice their opinions. In general, we still hold seniority as the most significant factor in determining compensation, but through the years we have adjusted the process to allow consideration of many other factors that may be subjectively weighed and taken into account.

We don't know how many other firms keep the number of hours billed and the fees collected known only to the billing lawyer, but we know from our own perspective that this practice is highly correlated with our personal satisfaction in the practice of law. Not disclosing billable hours and not basing compensation on fees is treasured by more than ninety percent of the lawyers in our firm. We think that it is one of the reasons that there is an exceptionally high degree of individual satisfaction with being a lawyer here, as measured by two anonymous surveys we have taken. Undoubtedly, the absence of billing pressure and jealousy over credit for a client and our trust in each lawyer are among the factors that lead to our high degree of career satisfaction.

So far, we have managed to keep the concepts of "eat what you kill" or "I brought this client to the firm and deserve a larger percentage of the fee," from influencing the discussions about sharing the firm's income. If there is some discussion of these factors, they are not decisive. Over time we have learned to trust that our lawyers will choose stimulating work. We try to remember that the generous legal fees in mergers and acquisitions may fade in an economic downturn, and litigation, the harbinger of troubled times, may be in the ascendancy. By taking the long view, we have been able to maintain a community that inspires our lawyers to reach their individual potential and to feel loyal to each other.

Our Clients

As part of our de-emphasis on billable hours, we try to develop in associates and younger partners the concept of value billing and how it benefits the law firm and the client. When we explain value billing to a client, it is always coupled with the clear assurance that any bill is subject to the client's complete approval and that the bill will always be adjusted as necessary so that the client is genuinely satisfied. This approach generally, but not always, appeals to clients, particularly to individual entrepreneurs. Large corporations, on the other hand, find it difficult to deviate from their custom of having fees calculated on the basis of billable hours.

Whether the arrangement with a client is based on billable hours or value billing, all lawyers in our firm keep a record of their time. In cases where the client insists on recorded hours as the basis of issuing a bill, the lawyer is in a position to submit a bill detailed in any manner the client may require. Time is one factor in the billing of any work done, but hourly billing does not automatically govern our relationships with our clients, just as it does not govern our relationships with each other. Over the long term, our emphasis on value billing instructs the younger persons in our firm that the practice of law is a true profession and that the essence of what we must offer clients is *value*.

More and more, we see evidence of clients beginning to realize that hourly billing may result in over-lawyering. Our experience with many clients over a period of time convinces us that they prefer a reasonable fee rather than a listing of hours worked. Their main lingering concern is that they have no yardstick as to what is reasonable. Our adherence to the factors in Rule 1.5 of South Carolina's Rules of Professional Conduct and, more important, our willingness to let the client have the last word on the subject of fees is an answer to their concern. This approach is not only a prescription for long range mutual satisfaction, but for mutual respect and, oftentimes, for abiding personal friendships.

A Principled Future

We have been fortunate that our firm has attracted lawyers with exceptional professional and academic credentials. We are proud that twelve of us have law degrees from Harvard; seven from the University of Virginia; and four from Yale. We also have law degrees from Vanderbilt, Columbia University, and the University of North Carolina. Ten of us are members of Phi Beta Kappa; two are members of Omicron Delta Kappa; one is a Rhodes Scholar; one is a MacArthur Fellow; and one is a Fulbright Scholar. Apart from our legal training, four lawyers have master degrees, one a doctorate, and one holds honorary doctorates from three schools. Twelve lawyers were members of law review. Four lawyers are members of the Order of Coif. Thirteen lawyers have clerked for the federal district court or court of appeals. Four lawyers have clerked in the United States Supreme Court.

In sharing these credentials, we hope to make the point that our long-established and cherished values and traditions have helped this small firm attract and retain some of the best-trained lawyers in the country.

We do not believe that our values and traditions are superior. There are good people who prefer structured, well-defined, even regimented arrangements. Natural dispositions, rather than financial ambition, may cause some lawyers to want greater discipline in their relationships. In fact, our experience is that some lawyers actually may be happier in a more regulated hierarchy in which the firm engages in a businesslike control over members' professional lives.

Our chief point is that the future of law firms will depend on whether the relationships among lawyers are founded on mutual trust and respect. We believe that every lawyer in our firm could be making substantially more money by joining a large firm in a large city, or by entering a different occupation, such as investment banking. Our lawyers make a conscious choice to join our firm because they are by and large seeking other rewards of practicing this profession than just financial success. The likelihood of their satisfaction is enhanced by the fact that the choice is made with an understanding of how we do things.

Except for the election of the Executive Committee, we have *never* voted on any matter. Our decisions are made by consensus. In reaching a consensus we sometimes resemble a meeting of Quakers. Everyone with a view speaks. Views may be predictable, but cliques rarely develop. With no votes to win or lose, decisions emerge fairly free from any alliances or hard feelings. The process may be, and often is, fairly slow and the issues are frequently reconsidered; however, it seems to capture the best of the deliberative process, without having winners and losers at the end.

We occasionally make adjustments in our firm's way of doing business to accommodate growth and diverse views. Up until now we have been able to make changes in ways that preserve our fundamental values. In a restatement of important principles unanimously adopted at a firm retreat in 1998, we described how we deal with change and with internal differences of opinion as follows:

> *We cherish the democratic nature of our firm decision-making, the diversity of opinion within the firm, and the right of each lawyer to speak on matters of concern to that individual. Our tradition of decision by a consensus of the whole has served us remarkably well over the years. Mutual respect demands that disagreement be discussed openly and directly. The fomenting of dissension and discontent behind the scenes is inimical to this culture.*

The past and the present have been good to our law firm. Our home, Greenville, South Carolina, has become an economic hot spot. Twenty years ago, Charlotte, North Carolina, was the size of Greenville today; at the present growth rate of Greenville, it probably will be less than 20 years before we reach the current size of Charlotte.

Our firm remains optimistic about the future because, to some extent, we believe that our small size gives us added ability to shape our future. Contrary to popular thinking, small law firms handle most of the legal business that is conducted in the United States every year, and most lawyers work in small law firms. Consequently, small firms may have an advantage because of their size. With fewer people, these firms have a better opportunity to build cohesive and strong internal and external relationships. Moreover, technology places small and large firms on a substantially equal footing in the ability to access and use knowledge; we feel that we can handle complex legal transactions as well as firms with many more lawyers than ours. Of course, none of these advancements will matter if our firm begins to value economic results more than our relationships with each other.

In the face of obvious and profound changes in the practice of law, at firm retreats we will continue to assess whether or not we need to adjust some aspects of our firm's way of doing business in order to preserve the traditions and principles that have guided us for so long. In the end, we continue to reaffirm our long-held values. If we can continue to do this while growing ever so modestly, our future and the future of all principle-centered law firms, regardless of their size, will be what it used to be - and better!

It was a common thing for Lincoln to discourage unnecessary lawsuits, and consequently he was constantly sacrificing opportunities to make money. One man who asked him to bring suit for two dollars and a half against a debtor who had not a cent with which to pay, would not be put off in his passion for revenge. His counsel therefore gravely demanded ten dollars as a retainer. Half of this he gave to the poor defendant, who thereupon confessed judgment and paid the $2.50. Thus, the suit was ended, to the entire satisfaction of the angry creditor.

Excerpt from "Lincoln's Own Stories"
by Anthony Gross (1912)

The Ideal Law Job

Steve Mendelsohn*

When I was graduating law school, all I wanted was a job that would let me do good law, would give me courtroom experience quickly, wouldn't require me to work long hours, and would pay well. Was that so much to ask?

The way I see it, there are three types of law: good law, bad law, and neutral law. Good law is doing good for society and having a "positive influence" on the world. For example, suing chemical companies that recklessly dump toxic waste into our water supply is good law. When I was selecting law firms, I purposely tried to interview with firms that do environmental law, so that I could help make the world a cleaner, safer place by suing the polluting chemical companies.

I was disgusted when I found out that the vast majority of those supposed "environmental law" firms actually defend chemical companies. That's not

---

* In addition to practicing law, Steve Mendelsohn "practices family" with his wife Lynn Siegel and their two children, Lauren and Jack.

environmental law; that's pollution law. Obviously, pollution law is bad law.

I consider patent law to be neutral law; that is, law that does neither good nor bad for society as a whole. It's just helping a bunch of engineers and businessmen who want to protect their inventions and investments. It's not exactly Mother Teresa, but it's not Al Capone either.

As a new law school graduate, I wanted to do good law. I would have settled for doing neutral law, but I wouldn't do bad law.

When I started my legal career, I also thought that I might want to be a courtroom lawyer. Earlier, I had learned that a courtroom lawyer is called a litigator. Soon after that, I learned that not all litigators are courtroom lawyers. Some litigators spend the first three or four years of their careers in the library writing briefs and memos, or sifting through boxes and boxes of interrogatory responses and depositions that someone else prepared or conducted. After two years, maybe these "litigators" get to watch a deposition.

Of course, every firm I interviewed with told me the same thing: "Here at Kiepum, Loctup, & Owtasite, you'll be given as much responsibility as you can handle, just as quickly and as early in your career as you make it happen." Why didn't I believe them? Maybe it's for the same reason that I never bother to open letters from publishing companies saying that I've already won.

In the early 1990s, Philadelphia firms expected associates to log from 1800 to 2250 billable hours per year. The way I figured it, even with only two weeks vacation, 2250 hours per year works out to an average of 45 billable hours per week. If you add in an hour for lunch and maybe an hour each day of non-billable schmoozing time, I'd have to be at work from eight in the morning till seven at night. Taking into account an hour to get ready in the morning, an hour for commuting each way, and the seven hours of sleep I needed to avoid being completely worthless, that left three whole hours each day. And that included dinner. What kind of a life is that?

Before going to law school, I had a master's degree in electrical engineering and six years of work experience. Don't tell anyone, but one of the reasons I went to law school was that, even in 1991, first-year associates were being paid more than an engineer with a master's degree and six years of work experience.

My First Job

I started my full-time professional legal career as an associate at a large general-practice law firm in

Philadelphia, assigned to its "neutral" patent law department.

I soon learned that there are two types of patent law. There's boring patent law, and then there's *really* boring patent law. Boring patent law is patent litigation. Really boring patent law is patent prosecution, which is Patentese for helping inventors get patents for their inventions. A patent prosecutor translates from Engineeringese, a language unfamiliar to most lawyers, into Patentese, an obscure dialect of Legalese.

As a new associate, I participated in the firm's admirable pro bono program, through which I was assigned to represent a plumber who was being sued by a neighbor for whom he had done work. I liked my client and was convinced that he was right, that the neighbor was lying, and that my client should win. Unfortunately, the arbitrators in the Philadelphia Court of Common Pleas, applying their version of Solomonic justice, decided to split the difference.

During that time, I was also the junior associate assigned to a litigation team defending another law firm accused of committing legal malpractice. The charges were ludicrous, and the plaintiffs' attorneys were jerks. Unfortunately, the jurors, applying their version of demonic justice, awarded the plaintiffs millions of dollars, of which the plaintiffs' lawyers undoubtedly received at least a third.

Despite having spent my entire life being argumentative, it was then that I realized for the first time that I like *meaningless* argument, not *meaningful* argument. I like arguing for the sake of arguing, not when someone's money or liberty is at stake; that's too much pressure for me. I never learned the lesson that I am sure most litigators learn: how to avoid getting emotionally involved in their clients' cases. I hate injustice and, if injustice is going to be done, then I'd rather not have to watch. And so, I got all of the litigation experience I needed fairly quickly in my career.

When I started as an associate at that large general-practice firm, I was required to log 1800 billable hours per year. My first full year as an associate doing mostly litigation, I was able to bill 2100 hours. However, as my workload slowly shifted from litigation to patent prosecution, it became harder and harder to rack up those kinds of hours. As I did more and more patent prosecution, I had to work longer and longer hours just to log the same number of billable hours. To make matters worse, the firm kept raising the billable hour requirement.

In the six years that I was an associate working in that large general-practice firm, a knot of Gordian proportions grew in the pit of my stomach. Every waking moment and even some sleeping ones were accompanied by a specific conscious awareness that time was divided into billable minutes and non-billable minutes, minutes that counted toward my annual bogey, and minutes that were wasted. Time spent eating and socializing felt like wasted minutes. Sure I ate, sure I socialized, but the knot was there, keeping me from really relaxing and enjoying myself. Even now, as I write these words, I can remember what that knot felt like and how it prevented me from both taking in a really deep breath and letting one all the way out.

One reason that I started my career at a large firm is that I figured it would be easier to move laterally from a large firm to a small firm than the other way around. Since I wasn't sure where I would be happier, I thought the prudent thing to do would be to start at a large firm and then, if things didn't work out, I could always move to a small firm.

Oh, yeah, I almost forgot to mention that the large firm was paying a better salary than I could get at a small firm. It was a lot of money for someone whose only skill was knowing how to draw with a Hi-Liter® marker without going outside the lines.

The Discovery

I am happy to announce that I eventually found the ideal law job. No, I'm not referring to the small patent firm I moved to as a six-year associate. That didn't work out the way I had hoped either. I'm referring to the law firm I started at the beginning of 1999, Mendelsohn & Associates, P.C.

Here at Mendelsohn & Associates, P.C., we do a lot of patent prosecution work, a smattering of trademark prosecution work, and not much else. I never go to court. I never file motions. I never take depositions, and I never even prepare interrogatories. For those of you who do these things and regard those of us who do not as not being real lawyers, let me just say this: I admit it; I'm not a real lawyer.

Most of our work is fixed-fee work. Associates are paid according to a formula that is based on the dollars billed, plus an additional bonus for bringing in new clients. Most importantly, there are no billable hour requirements. As long as an associate covers his or her share of the expenses, he or she gets to decide how hard to work. The more you work, the more money you earn. It's all carrot and no stick.

Every day at Mendelsohn & Associates, P.C., is a "dress-down Friday." I never go to court and my engineer clients won't talk to me if I visit them wearing a suit. I do, however, have a suit hanging on our coat rack just in case I need to go to a bar association meeting and pretend that I am a real lawyer.

At Mendelsohn & Associates, P.C., lawyers work when and where they want. I work at home at least one day a week. There is no specified limit for vacation time. As long as deadlines are met, I don't care how much vacation an associate takes. Since almost all of the work we do is for fixed fees, for the most part, I don't even keep track of the time I spend. There are no timesheets and no knots in my stomach.

Our clients are inventors, who are almost by definition of above average intelligence. At the very least, they are inventive. It's all ex parte work, so we never have to deal with "opposing counsel." The examiners at the patent office act as judges determining the patentability of our clients' inventions, except that, unlike judges, most examiners are reasonable people. They're just engineers themselves who are simply trying to do the right thing.

The shortest deadline dictated by the patent office is two months and most deadlines are three months. Even then, you can buy as many as three additional months in which to respond if you need more time. It's a little easier to have a life when the biggest crisis is figuring out how to squeeze in an extra day's worth of work over the next fiscal quarter to meet a patent office deadline.

So, after searching for almost 10 years, I have finally found the ideal law job. At least, I've found *my* ideal law job. It's not the same ideal law job that I was looking for when I started my legal career, and it may not be my ideal law job tomorrow. But if I ever become dissatisfied with my *current* ideal law job, I know I'll do whatever it takes to begin another search to find my *next* ideal law job.

Every life is a profession of faith, and exercises an inevitable and silent influence.

Henri Frederic Amiel

True Mentoring

George W. Kaufman*

When I graduated law school in 1962, I had very little sense of who I was or how my career might unfold. Luckily, Walter Petschek became my mentor. He was the senior corporate partner of my first employer, Rosenman & Colin. Although he was an expert in a broad range of subjects with a particular affinity for trusts and estates, the things I learned from him went far beyond matters of law.

For example, when I had been at the firm for six months, I received an assignment to draft a complicated will for one of our long term clients. After a week of non-stop drafting, I submitted some seventy pages to Walter's secretary. The next day the will was back on my desk, filled with comments and corrections. My ego was deflated. I spent the day deciphering Walter's

---

* George W. Kaufman has been a practicing lawyer since 1962. He is the author of "The Lawyer's Guide To Balancing Life And Work: Taking The Stress Out Of Success." Mr. Kaufman serves as Vice-Chair of the Omega Institute, the largest holistic retreat facility in the United States. He teaches and writes frequently on the subject of mentoring and the challenge of how to balance our professional and personal lives.

queries and formulating a half dozen questions I wanted to ask him.

Early that next morning, I waited at his door with my questions in hand. Walter came to work at 8 a.m. sharp, every morning. It was quiet at that hour, and a good time to get his full attention. He patiently explained what I hadn't grasped, and sent me on my way. Unfortunately, I still didn't understand one of his answers. So, with some trepidation I went back to see him the next morning.

This time, his patience was thinner. I blurted out my remaining question and pointed to the place in the will that still confused me. He grabbed the papers from me and looked at them. His thick white eyebrows cascaded over the frame of his glasses, as he read.

After what seemed like an interminable wait, he barked at me, "Do you know why you don't understand what I told you?" Lots of reasons came to mind, but none that seemed wise to share just then. Without waiting for my response, he eased back, thought for a moment, and said, "Because what I told you was wrong. You had it right."

It was an epiphany. Walter could be wrong, I could be right, and he was still the teacher! What I learned about will drafting has long since faded, but the notion of teaching by fallibility was an indelible lesson. It didn't make him less capable, just more human. It meant that I could be human too.

In contrast to my early days in law, our profession is currently in trouble. The roots of our problem can be found in the dissatisfaction that so many lawyers experience while practicing their craft. Part of the problem is that today's young lawyers have few models to draw upon and receive little comfort from their seniors. Intimate conversations that lead to changes in jobs or careers are usually reserved for families and therapists, rather than other attorneys who actually have the experience that young lawyers need to hear.

I believe that a return to a tradition of mentoring can greatly improve the state of our profession. It is the best way I know of to teach two crucial elements of a satisfying career in law: *values and connectivity*. When I refer to values, I mean those human qualities that describe who we are at our best moments. By connectivity, I mean understanding the importance of fostering relationships with each other.

Values

I want to share with you five values that are important for a mentor to incorporate into daily life and to use as core elements of any relationship created with a protégé:

- Authenticity
- Commitment
- Humility
- Integrity
- True Listening

Authenticity is achieved by understanding who we are and making life choices consistent with that knowledge. To illustrate the point, let me share a tale with you about a Hasidic rabbi musing over a conversation he fantasizes having with God in the next life. The rabbi tells his congregation:

"If God asks me why in this life I hadn't lived more like Isaac, or Abraham or Moses, I will know how to respond. But if God asks me why in this life I hadn't lived more like me, I will have nothing to say."

To affirm my views about authenticity, let me share one of the last encounters I had with my mentor, Walter. Six months before I left the firm I needed some friendly advice. On a certain Monday morning at 8 a.m., I came to Walter's door. He looked up from his desk, and asked me what I wanted.

"A personal matter," I confessed.

"Come back at six tonight," Walter responded. The conversation was over. His pencil danced across the pages of the newest associate's effort to master will writing.

I returned at six that night. "Close the door," he said. I did and then sat down at the long table he used for a desk. Without saying a word, Walter reached behind the desk and found two glasses and a bottle of scotch. He poured generously into both glasses. "Shoot" he said, and sat back. Two hours later I left.

Walter had leveled the playing field and invited me to roam over the whole landscape of the profession, to talk about my options, to explore my working as a principal in a small business, and to ask whether I would be invited back if I left.

"What lawyer hasn't thought of leaving?" Walter asked. He had been trained as a mining engineer and knew something about career changes. His candor was refreshing and his availability was a thank you for the nights and weekends I had spent on his corporate mergers. In the end I left, but I left with his blessing and the door still open.

Over the years, I served as an officer and partner in business and the law, and counseled scores of associates and employees on choices about their future. My guide for each of those encounters was based on that single intervention by Walter. Minus the scotch, I have tried to emulate his candor, openness, and support.

In addition to authenticity, there is another fundamental aspect to mentoring: the level of commitment that the mentor and protégé are willing to bring to the relationship. Commitments can be expressed in many ways.

Here is a story that exemplifies one form of commitment. In 16th century China, at the height of the Samurai era, one of its famous warriors approached a Buddhist sage and insisted that he teach him about heaven and hell. "I am in a hurry, old man, so do it quickly," said the warrior.

The old man looked up at his unexpected visitor and laughed. "Teach you?" he said. "I would sooner teach a pig. You are ill mannered, boorish, and a lout. You smell, you're thoughtless, and you are a blot to humanity."

As this stinging rebuke was uttered, the Samurai's complexion turned to purple. Rage consumed him, that this small, insignificant speck of humanity would dare to impugn the honor of a great warrior. In a flash, he unsheathed his sword and raised it high to end the worthless life of the priest, who sat before him, unmoving.

In the moment before the sword made its swift descent, the priest locked eyes with the Samurai and said quietly, "That which you are now feeling is Hell."

The Samurai was shocked by the message. The priest had risked his own life to provide an instant lesson. Had the Samurai not heard him, or not listened, the priest's life would be gone. This man had been willing to risk his own being to teach the Samurai the lessons he had requested.

Gently, the Samurai laid his sword at the feet of the priest. Overcome, he began to cry. "And that", said the priest gently, "is Heaven."

In my second year at Yale Law School, Fritz Kessler was my teacher for contracts law. Fritz had escaped from Nazi Germany and became a dedicated law professor, with an obvious enthusiasm for teaching his students. One afternoon, in a moment of excitement, Fritz exclaimed to his students, "You must read this case. YOU MUST!" His voice had a note of urgency, his hands had punched the air for emphasis, and his entire being had reflected his vibrancy.

Then, leaning on the podium from which he taught, Fritz softened his voice and, obviously embarrassed, told us: "You see, it may not be exciting to you, but for me, it's my life." And then Fritz blushed. Confessions of the heart don't come easily to lawyers. The experience was not lost on anyone in his class. His fire was contagious. His enthusiasm was evident.

One year, Fritz took a leave of absence from Yale and taught at Harvard on an exchange program. On the first day of classes, Fritz was assigned to lecture in one of Harvard's large auditoriums and made a silly joke. The Harvard students, true to their law school tradition, hissed in unison at his bad pun.

Fritz looked up in surprise, not understanding their reaction. Then, as he realized it was just a tradition, he smiled, and in his thick accent told the students, "You know, dat's vat ze snake said to Eve." For that response, Fritz got a standing ovation and the hearts of his Harvard students.

Years later, when I felt bogged down in my daily practice, I yearned for his passion and his devotion to students. Fritz wasn't just a dedicated teacher. He was dedicated to teaching. Being dedicated to teaching assumes a larger vision, a sustaining belief in the commitment of the value that teaching serves.

In my years of practice, the matters I handled had their share of peak experiences and deep troughs. The composite of those years are formed from moments of singular disappointment and shared joy. I was dedicated, but unable to feel the passion Fritz had experienced when he uttered "You see, it's my life."

As I began to explore my own frustrations with practicing law, I looked at patterns I shared in common with many other lawyers. Eventually, I created a program that served lawyers by helping them find a voice for their deepest passions. Those seminars, and the book it eventually spawned, were a service I could practice with fire. Instead of withdrawing from the field of law, I became committed to working within it. Gandhi advised us "to be the change we want to see in the world." Fritz would have agreed.

Another important value a mentor can encourage in a protégé is *humility*. Lawyers are not ego deficient. The structure of our practice feeds this part of human nature and we find ourselves constantly in competition. Winning expands our egos and losing shrinks them back down in size. Over time, our paychecks may grow, our offices get larger, our responsibilities multiply, and our titles increase. These trappings have seductive qualities about them. The more success we experience as lawyers the more we stand out in that community as a somebody.

The author, Ram Dass, found the process quite similar when he was a young psychologist teaching at Harvard. As he noted, "I was becoming a somebody, and I was living in somebody land." The danger of course is that if we become a somebody, we will behave in a way driven by our desire to maintain that status. We will confuse trappings with essence and information with knowledge.

We have all heard the expression that a person is full of himself. When we use that expression, we mean that the person has no room to allow other people or other experiences to come into his life. That fullness creates a barrier, and so long as that barrier exists, learning is blocked. In true mentoring, the mentor as well as the protégé have a great deal to learn. But if the mentor is too filled with his degrees and his status, too full of himself, he has no room left to learn. The mentor will not be able to hear what the protégé needs and the interconnection between the two will die.

A true mentor also models *integrity*. We think of mentoring as a conscious act between the mentor and protégé. All our actions, however, not just the conscious ones, are influential. Imagine driving your car with your son in the front seat next to you. Suddenly a car swerves in front of you, nearly causing an accident. You roll down the window as you pull up alongside the offending car, screaming and cursing at the careless driver. Are you mentoring your child at that moment? Even though you are exhibiting behavior you would rather he didn't, your son takes it all in.

Early in my career, I worked directly with clients on immigration matters. Even though the matters were small, it was a heady experience doing direct representation. One client I worked with was the treasurer of a real estate corporation. He wanted to bring a cook from eastern Europe to his home in the United States. All went well until I told the client that the process took about three months. Any rapport I had established with the client instantly vanished.

"Three months my ass," he screamed. "If I wanted her here in three months, I could have used anybody. I want her here in three weeks."

My next stop was Walter's office. The client was Walter's, though I wasn't too sure for how long. Walter had me walk him through the conversation, including all the details. Then he made sure I was right on my timetable. After he was fully informed, Walter told me that he would take care of the client and that I should take care of the immigration work, no matter how long it took to bring the cook to America.

As far as Walter was concerned, we would not consider pulling strings or using influence. If the client didn't like the advice we gave him, he could try another firm. I completed the matter and, three months later, the cook entered the United States as an employee of the client.

That type of mentoring constantly went on with Walter. No words were ever exchanged about the moral dilemma posed. There was a right way to proceed and Walter intended to follow it.

Finally, another value that a mentor can foster in a protégé is *true listening*. Harville Hedricks, author of *Getting the Love You Want*, tells about a couple he is counseling. The husband, a self confident and assured lawyer, is sharing with Harville a recent family argument. Harville interrupts, telling them both to listen to a piece of music he wants to play. When it finishes, Harville asks each to tell him what they heard.

The wife speaks about the piano and how it creates a stormy backdrop for the piece. The husband disagrees violently. After naming the composer, he proceeds to give a textbook analysis of the music, relegating the brooding overtones to an afterthought. Then Harville asks them to listen again, but this time to listen for what the other person must have heard in offering their description.

The husband is dumbfounded. He had listened often to the piece, but never paid attention to the piano. Now that he does, he can hear what his wife has heard. Through this simple exercise, Harville created a non-toxic way for the husband and wife to be in each other's shoes. By inviting them to listen from another's person's point of view, Harville had begun the process of teaching this couple how to dissolve their separateness.

People want most to be heard and understood. Offering your attention to another person is a critical part of any mentoring process. If you mentor younger lawyers, you must give them your attention. What will eventually tumble out are their feelings and their confusion. We have been trained to guard our feelings, to suppress our emotions in favor of our intellect, to hide our vulnerability, and to shield our weaknesses. If we deliver those messages to our protégés, they will not find in us what they are seeking and the relationship will sputter.

Even if you cannot give answers to the feelings swirling inside protégés, you can honor their authenticity. Generally those feelings have an anger component you can either stifle or allow to come to the surface. When given the chance to breathe, that anger is often masking old and deep rooted fears. And it is in those fears where our vulnerability dwells.

Listening requires safety. As the mentor, it's your responsibility to make sure that what is said between you and the person you engage with remains confidential. Without safety nothing will happen. When people don't feel safe, you only hear guarded comments.

Connectivity

In the nature of how we practice law, many of our daily interactions are antagonistic. On behalf of our clients, we serve in the role of advocates. Whether we're sitting in our law offices, appearing in a courtroom, or negotiating across the table from other lawyers, our advocacy is often strident; we exploit differences, measure performances, personalize matters and practice isolating behaviors. Too often our advocacy is stretched beyond acceptable boundaries. In the process, we attenuate our ability to find connections.

I remember watching Muhammed Ali fight Joe Frazier. Two talented men pummeling each other for fifteen rounds within the rules that govern boxing. At the end of the fight, they hugged and held on to each other in a show of respect and affection. Each admired the skills the other possessed. Neither sought to win in a manner that would disgrace either of them. Both recognized the person being fought was more a partner than an opponent. Each needed someone of sufficient fighting skill to allow the talents of the other to emerge.

The advocacy I am railing against is the advocacy that is mean spirited, fueled by anger and a callous indifference to human qualities. In 1954 The U.S. Senate conducted what are remembered as the Army-McCarthy hearings. Joseph Welch was the lawyer for different persons in the Army that had been called to testify in those hearings. The McCarthy staff sought to embarrass Welch by exposing one of his aides as a homosexual.

When the disclosure was finished, Welch was furious at the level to which the McCarthy staff had sunk in making that disclosure. In a statement that has remained a classic in the annals of legal interaction, Welch stood up, pointed his finger at Joseph McCarthy, and said "Sir, have you no shred of decency left in you at all?"

Welch was the hero of those hearings. What made him a hero was his decency in the face of risk. His compassion for a distraught staff aide created an electrifying moment. In our profession we have very few heroes and very few heroic moments. When people recall those hearings, no one remembers how Welch performed as a lawyer. They remember how he performed as a human being.

We have about a million members in our profession. Too many of us act as though we don't share common roots, and practice without any regard to nurturing the environment in which we work. We have become hardened by the work we do, the demands of our clients, the stridency of our opponents, and the tugs of our own colleagues.

Eli Wiesel said that the opposite of love is not hate; it's indifference. In practicing law, too many of us have become a reflection of indifferent behavior. The indifference we practice is a protection we wrap around ourselves. It modulates our stress and suppresses the feelings that accumulate from the constant pressures to perform. While our indifference may appear to be a form of professional demeanor, it reveals the lack of spirit or enthusiasm we bring to work.

How can we infuse spirit back into our work? We need to recognize that we are a community bonded by our common agreement to serve the law. The form that our service takes has the potential to bind us closer together or split us further apart. It certainly is within our power to support each other should we seek to emphasize the community aspects of our profession. The support that I believe would be most helpful, springs from mentoring programs.

Years ago I met a man on the local bus traveling into the town of Cruz Bay on St. John's Island, a part of the U.S. Virgin Islands. We talked as we rode. Rick shared with me that, as a youngster, he was going down a bad path when a stranger took him into his home for a month. On the day he was leaving to return home, the stranger asked how he intended to pay for his month's stay.

Rick was in shock. "What are you talking about?" asked Rick . "I don't have any money, and you know that. I'm broke."

The stranger was adamant. "You slept in my bed, ate my food and used my house for a whole month. I don't want your money, but you need to pay and I'm going to tell you how. By the time you're forty, I want you to do for ten kids what I just did for you."

Rick laughed. "It took me until I was forty-five. And every time a kid gets ready to leave I ask him, "How are you going to pay me?"

As mentors, we have the capacity to work with younger attorneys who are uncomfortable in their current law practices. We could, for example, agree to invite just one attorney a year into a mentoring relationship with us. In that manner, we can build a cadre of caring lawyers who accept supporting other lawyers as part of their job description.

If each of us takes responsibility for facilitating the needs of others, our profession will develop into a caring community and a place of belonging that we're proud of rather than merely tolerate. Through this approach we not only teach each other, but we support each other. The internal dividend will be a heightened reverence in our daily practice and the external dividend will be a societal shift in how the public views our profession.

The mentoring process is not just about helping others, but also about helping ourselves. We need to be softer on ourselves. We need to allow room for mistakes, for errors, and for fallibility. If we can embrace these imperfections we will begin to make room for the qualities we want to reflect.

I am suggesting that it's time to create mentoring programs designed around relationship rather than information. There is no way to know the degree to which such an effort will impact the legal community, but we do know that our current interactions aren't working well. We need a very different conversation, one marked with the spirit to ignite our passions.

Let me share one final story with you. My friend Dave was a real estate lawyer who took a position with a prominent New York law firm. He worked for a senior partner named Fred, who had a reputation for being tenacious, short tempered and impatient. Dave had barely been at the firm two years when he was diagnosed with a cancer that would prove to be fatal. Still, Dave came to work through his illness and through his treatment. Near the end of his life, it took Dave longer to get to his office and became increasingly harder to turn out productive work.

As Dave's deterioration became visible, Fred called Dave into his office. He said to him: "Go home. Fight your illness. Take care of yourself. Your job will be waiting for you, no matter how long it takes. Come back when you're able."

Dave never made it back. But he took home with him Fred's message of a job well done that would continue to pay him until he died. Fred overrode his personal needs and the needs of his firm, in favor of supporting another human being. Dave was no longer being seen as a profit center, but as a person that Fred could help. Fred's simple act of kindness connected him with his protégé in a way that served them both.

A year and a half after Dave died, I had lunch with his wife. Of all the experiences she remembered about Dave's work as a lawyer, Fred's behavior was paramount.

In Conclusion

The concept of mentoring came to us from Greek mythology. When Odysseus left for war, he asked his friend and advisor, Mentor, to serve as the guardian and teacher of his son, Telemachus. Odysseus entrusted the training of the person he held most dear to another person. In selecting Mentor, Odysseus picked someone whose values matched his own and who embodied qualities Odysseus knew were essential to pass on.

It is no surprise that mentoring as a two thousand year old practice has undergone some dilution. What remains at the core, however, is the seriousness of what's being undertaken for both the mentor and the protégé. Becoming a mentor can be an awesome responsibility and a sacred trust. It can also be one of the most fulfilling and important things you will ever do as a lawyer.

The Lawyer

Thomas D. Morse*

His order, ancient as the race,
A proud Republic stands;
Where Justice holds the highest place
And Mercy Folds her hands.

Historic Time proclaims his worth
On carven stone and page,
And how his wisdom wrought the birth
Of Equity's great age.

Wielding the blessing and the ban,
His is a lofty fame;
A High Priest in the Court of Man,
His tithe - a spotless name.

---

*Little is known about this poem or its author. The poem was published in 1900, in a book entitled "The Lawyer's Cove: Poems by the Lawyer, for the Lawyer and about the Lawyer," which was edited by Ina Russelle Warren. The book was reprinted in 1990 under the editorship of J. Wesley Miller. Two other good legal poetry books published in the 1800s were entitled "Poems of the Law" and "Lyrics of the Law."

A weaver of life's tapestry,
He sees the shuttle glide,
And learns the human misery
That mars the hidden side.

The World pours in his ear her tale
Of sorrow, sin, and shame;
His confidence, a sacred veil,
E'er guards it as a flame.

Powers and Thrones have known him well,
The anchor and the stay,
Whose sovran genius wrought the spell
That saved the State alway.

Maligned, misused, least understood
Of all earth's good and great,
Still true, he guides a thankless brood,
As passionless as Fate.

And when he stands, as stand he must,
In the Great High Court above,
His only plea, "Lord God, be just,
Adjudge, decree in love."

Lawyers From The School Of Athens

Mark R. Siwik*

Happiness and joy have disappeared from the lives of many lawyers. For a time, the same thing happened to me. Early in my career, my wife would tell me that she hated Sundays because, on this supposed day of rest, I was restless. I could not stop thinking about my work. What if there was one more relevant case to find? Had I anticipated and addressed all possible arguments?

Sundays meant that my short reprieve from legal work was over. When I entered the office early the next morning, there would be more questions, more issues, and more problems. Above all else, I was angry. I was angry because I went to law school to make a difference. I wanted to change things. I wanted to help people. I started to believe that I wasn't making a difference and that hurt most of all.

Over time, I learned that many other lawyers felt the same way. I learned that the legal profession had

---

* Mark R. Siwik is Senior Counsel at Risk International Services, Inc., where he helps commercial policyholders resolve complex insurance claims. He was formerly a partner with the firm of Brouse McDowell. Mark also devotes substantial time to speaking to and working with lawyers on improving the legal profession.

high rates of depression and substance abuse. In fact, things were so bad that all the lawyers in my state were required to receive regular education on substance abuse. Fortunately, I did not develop a substance abuse problem, but I began to question whether this type of training was the right approach. Where was the training to attack the root of the problems in the legal profession, which in turn lead to substance abuse?

I wanted something more than the instruction "don't drink." I wanted something more positive that might help me make good decisions and recapture that lost optimism and idealism that led me to become a lawyer in the first place.

Not finding that type of training in continuing legal education programs, I began reading various books and articles. They confirmed my diagnosis that the legal profession was in trouble and often suggested that the only viable antidote was to leave the law. Since I did not want to leave the law, I kept expanding my reading list.

I don't remember when, but at some point the reading made me think about a painting I had not seen in years. I first saw *The School of Athens* when I was a freshman in college, but now I couldn't even remember the title and my visual memory of it had grown faint. I dusted off my college textbooks looking for the painting in vain. Finally, the staff at the Cleveland Art Museum helped me remember the title of the painting and directed me to a store in New York. I bought a print, framed it, and hung it in my office.

Created by Raphael as a mural for the Vatican's papal library nearly 500 years ago, *The School of Athens* is an allegory of human knowledge. It depicts many eminent Greek thinkers such as Plato, Aristotle, Socrates, Pythagoras, and Euclid, within a majestic architectural background. Since Raphael could not have known what his subjects looked like, he used the faces of various artists of his time, including himself, Michelangelo and Leonardo da Vinci.

The fresco weaves together images of humanity's most important earthly contributions, such as art, science, and philosophy. It illustrates the continuity of thought, and how much the future owes to the present, which in turn is built upon the past. It also expresses a sense of majesty and balance.

For me, the painting is a symbolic message of what it takes to lead a successful and satisfying life. Every time I look at the painting, I see a blueprint for constructing a life that produces a meaningful legacy. Although I didn't appreciate it at the time, it is clear now that I returned to *The School of Athens* because I had lost my way.

How did I lose my way? I think it began in law school. For most of the first year, law school was like riding a roller coaster. The process of reading countless legal opinions to prepare for a cross examination by an experienced professor was grueling. I alternated between periods of fatigue, intellectual stimulation, and raw fear. The second and third years of law school were better, as I became more comfortable with the Socratic method of teaching, and developed some practical skills like negotiation and advocacy.

Still, something was missing. I did not leave law school with a clear sense of myself or how to pursue my vocation in a way that would make me feel fulfilled. For all the wonderful law school training I had received, I am fairly certain that it bore little resemblance to the true Socratic method. The Socrates standing in Raphael's painting frequently asked his students the types of questions that never came up in my legal training: "Who are you? What kind of person will you become?" These questions were not asked of me in law school.

A hundred years ago, Oliver Wendell Holmes, asked the same types of questions of his audiences. Appearing before bar associations, Holmes asked the lawyers of his day how they intended to make out a fulfilling life when at times it might seem that law was nothing more than "the laborious study of a dry and technical system, the greedy watch for clients, the practice of shopkeepers arts, and the mannerless conflicts over often sordid interests." His answer was: "If the lawyer has the soul of Sancho Panza, the world to that lawyer will be Sancho Panza's world; but if the lawyer has the soul of an idealist, the lawyer will make — I do not say find — his or her world ideal."

Eventually, I realized that part of my problem was that I had no plan to make my world ideal. I had not defined success for myself or decided how I would create a meaningful life.

As I worked through these issues, I learned the importance of balancing idealism with realism. This lesson is conveyed by the way the philosophers are organized in *The School of Athens.* Plato and Aristotle stand in the middle of the painting. Plato represents idealism and he is shown raising his finger to the heavens. Surrounding Plato is the statue of Apollo, the god of poetry, and Pythagoras, who is writing his philosophy of life according to the harmonic proportions of music. Aristotle represents realism and is seen lowering one hand to the earth and holding his book of Ethics in the other hand. He is surrounded by prominent mathematicians and scientists, and the statue of Minerva, representing intelligence.

In my mind, Plato and Aristotle represent two aspects of the path to success: Plato moving from the reality of earth to the ideal and Aristotle intent on finding the ideal in this world. Together, they teach us to succeed by using both our hearts and our minds.

Applying this simple perspective to my life has not been easy. In law school, I began to lose my ability to heed my heart. I honed my analytical skills to the point of being able to argue either side of an issue with ease, partly by setting aside my personal feelings and conscience. When I entered the profession, if a client asked me for representation, I felt duty bound to zealously advocate his or her position, regardless of how I felt. I also found myself always needing to have the right answer and to win every point, even those which were insignificant.

I now know that my life needs equal amounts of idealism and realism. United States Supreme Court Justice Felix Frankfurter put it this way in response to a young person who asked him for advice on how to become a lawyer:

> *No one can be a truly competent lawyer unless he is a cultivated [person]. If I were*

you I would forget all about any technical preparation for the law. The best way to prepare for the law is to come to the study of the law as a well-read person. Thus alone can one acquire the capacity to use the English language on paper and in speech and with the habits of clear thinking which only a truly liberal education can give. No less important for a lawyer is the cultivation of the imaginative faculties by reading poetry, seeing great paintings, in the original or in easily available reproductions, and listening to great music. Stock your mind with the deposit of much good reading, and widen and deepen your feelings by experiencing vicariously as much as possible the wonderful mysteries of the universe, and forget all about your future career.

Frankfurter understood that a truly capable lawyer is, at bottom, a well-rounded person. With a fully developed mind and heart, the lawyer is able to meet his or her own deepest needs as well as those of others. In turn, life is no longer a game which we try to win. Instead, life becomes the pursuit of an ethically satisfactory existence.

Because leading a quality life is challenging, I often look for inspiration in the lives of others. For example, I admire Benjamin Franklin's lifelong pursuit of moral perfection. As a young adult, Franklin developed a list of twelve virtues from which he would try to build his character. Through the use of a journal, Franklin recorded his progress in trying to live his life in accordance with these virtues. Quite proud of his invention, he shared his journal with a Quaker friend who politely informed Franklin that he was a poor listener and that he could be insolent when making a point. Endeavoring to break this habit, Franklin added the virtue of humility to his list. Then, in a moment which undoubtedly earned him a place in *The School of Athens*, Franklin defined humility as the practice of imitating Jesus and Socrates.

Borrowing from Franklin's example, I try to take the long view. Sometimes when I feel myself losing patience, I look at the part of the painting which depicts the life of a master artisan or craftsman. In the lower right hand corner of *The School of Athens,* appears the master of geometry, Euclid, who is working with four students, each of whom represent a different stage of learning. The first student, closest to the master and kneeling forward, is at the level of literal learning. Next to him is a student whose face shows the look of dawning comprehension. The third stage of learning is represented by the student who is gesturing because he knows the outcome of the exercise, and because he can see other applications. Finally, we see Euclid's apprentice who is encouraging the first student and is assisting Euclid in teaching the exercise.

"These are the stages I will pass through on my path to success," I think to myself. There are no short cuts. There is no substitute for working continuously to improve my character. As Socrates told us, only when we regularly examine our lives, do we create the possibility of pursuing a life worth living.

At some point, we gain the ability to expand our focus from ourselves to improving the world around us. As a profession, we are having a difficult time making our world ideal. Young lawyers work long days and nights to gain expertise and experience. Experienced lawyers compete with each other to grow their individual books of business. Senior lawyers worry about keeping a place in their firm. Too many lawyers go home each night, exhausted with little time or energy for their families. Some lawyers don't even feel it possible to be a lawyer and a parent and so they avoid family life altogether.

Public respect for the legal profession has never been lower. Much has changed since the 1830's when Alexis de Tocqueville wrote:

> *If you ask me where the American aristocracy is found, I have no hesitation in answering that it is not among the rich, who have no common link uniting them. It is at the bar or the bench that the American aristocracy is found. . . . When the American people let themselves get intoxicated by their passions or carried away by their ideas, the lawyers apply an almost invisible brake which slows them down. . . . Lawyers, forming the only enlightened class not distrusted by the people, are naturally called on to fill most public functions.*

In contrast to de Tocqueville's time, lawyers are now regarded as symbols of everything that is crass about American society.

"It does not have to be this way." That was the advice I heard in 1992 when I asked an instructor at a continuing legal education program how a young lawyer could remain optimistic in the face of so many problems confronting the legal profession.

What way should the profession be? All I can say is that it takes courage to try to make things better. "Each of us can work to change a small portion of events, and in the total of all those acts will be written the history of this generation." Robert Kennedy's words still ring true today. When each of us act, we send forth a "tiny ripple of hope" which can build a mighty current of change.

I want to see three changes occur in the legal profession. First, I hope that a new model of a professional service firm will emerge. Most existing models base compensation solely on collections and seniority which, in turn, has the practical effect of rewarding only the few at the top. Billable hours and leveraging are the words most often used to describe this model.

Under the new model, economics would still be an important factor, but it would not be the determining factor. Instead, the professionals would concentrate on establishing a common set of values which, in turn would become the bedrock of the firm's culture and the basis by which the individuals in the firm relate to each other and to their clients. These values would hold the firm together in the same way that principles hold Raphael's School of Athens together. Service and accountability to shared values would be the words most often used to describe this new model.

Second, I hope to see lawyers earn the love and respect they once had in their communities. If I could, I would make every lawyer read Harper Lee's self-described "simple love story," *To Kill a Mockingbird.* I want every lawyer to feel the consternation that little eight-year-old Jean Louise felt when she watched the adults of her world convict an innocent man. More importantly, I want every lawyer to feel the love and respect we all felt when Reverend Sykes whispered to Jean Louise as her lawyer-father left the courtroom: "Miss Jean Louise . . . Miss Jean Louise, stand up. Your father's passin."

What moves us all about *To Kill a Mockingbird* is the love and respect the community had for Atticus Finch even though he had lost the case. The community respected Atticus because they saw in him a human being whom they trusted to do the best he could in an imperfect world and imperfect legal system. The respect we want from the public will return when enough lawyers, in their own individual way, act in a manner worthy of such respect.

This brings me to my third and final aspiration for the legal profession. I hope that this generation and the next one produce a group of lawyers with the ability to create and sustain a fulfilling career in law and to serve society. The process of bringing about the necessary reforms for this to occur requires lawyers in powerful positions to help light the way. They must be willing to lead by example and in so doing, challenge the rest of us to learn to change. I can think of no finer place for this learning to occur than to return to the place where the legal profession began, *The School of Athens*.

Recommended Readings

Stress Management, Professionalism, And Other Self-Help Books For Lawyers

A. Elwork with contributions by D. B. Marlowe, *Stress Management For Lawyers: How to Increase Personal and Professional Satisfaction in the Law* (1997).

G. W. Kaufman, *The Lawyer's Guide To Balancing Life And Work: Taking The Stress Out Of Success* (1999).

S. Keeva, *Transforming Practices: Finding Joy And Satisfaction In The Legal Life* (1999).

M. Papantonio, *In Search of Atticus Finch: A Motivational Book for Lawyers*

B. Sells, *The Soul Of The Law* (1994).

Law Firm Management

D.H. Maister, *True Professionalism: The Courage to Care About Your People, Your Clients, and Your Career* (1997).

D.H. Maister, *Managing The Professional Service Firm* (1993).

Career Counseling for Lawyers

D. L. Arron, *What Can You Do With A Law Degree: A Lawyer's Career Guide to Career Alternatives Inside, Outside and Around Law* (1997).

H. Greenberg, *The Lawyer's Career Change Handbook: More Than 300 Things You Can Do With A Law Degree* (1998)

Time Management

S. R. Covey, A. R. Merrill and R. R. Merrill, *First Things First* (1994).

A. Mackenzie, *The Time Trap* (1990).

General Self-Improvement

S. R. Covey, *The 7 Habits Of Highly Effective People* (1989).

D. Goleman, *Working With Emotional Intelligence* (1998).

Dear Reader,

If this book has inspired you or influenced you in any way, please consider sharing your reaction, ideas and insights with us. Your feedback will help us continue to learn how to change things for the better.

Additionally, if you are interested in contributing a story, article or poem to books like this one in the future, please feel free to send it to:

Mark Siwik
Success Briefs Project, Suite 220
4199 Kinross Lakes Parkway
Richfield, OH 44286
Phone: (440) 463-5000
Fax: (440) 463-5050
msiwik@aol.com

Thank you,

Mark Siwik
Amiram Elwork

ORDER FORM

"SUCCESS BRIEFS FOR LAWYERS"
(ISBN # 0-9644727-2-4)

Please send me ______ copy (ies) at $26.95, with free regular shipping (takes 1-2 weeks). For Priority Mail shipping (3-4 days), write "RUSH" on form and add $4.00 for the first book and $1.00 for each additional book. Pennsylvania residents must pay a 6% sales tax. If ordering 6 or more copies, please call for information on volume discounts and shipping costs.

My total due is: $ __________

Ship Order To: ________________________________

____

____

Phone: ____________________________________

Payment by (circle): Check MasterCard VISA Amer.Exp.

Card# _ _ _ _ _ - _ _ _ _ _ - _ _ _ _ _ - _ _ _ _

Exp. Date: _ _ / _ _ Signature ____________________

Mail: The Vorkell Group, P.O. Box 447, Gwynedd, PA 19436

Fax: 215-661-9328 Telephone Voice Mail: 800-759-1222

Website: Vorkell.com

Also available through bookstores and the Internet.